AF334247

Discovery & Recognition

Discovery & Recognition

James Alinder

Editor

Untitled 25

The Friends of Photography

Acknowledgements

This issue of *Untitled* brings together diverse offerings that make fascinating viewing and reading. For their important help with the issue I would like to thank Harry Callahan; Lee Friedlander; Mark Klett; Ursula Gropper of the Grapestake Gallery; Richard Misrach; Peter MacGill, Marnie Gillett and Renato Danese of Light Gallery; Janet Borden and Robert Freidus of the Robert Freidus Gallery; Harry Lunn and Ron Hill of the Harry Lunn Gallery; Wright Morris; The American Scholar; Beaumont Newhall; Anita Mozley; the Stanford University Museum of Art; the Imogen Cunningham Trust; the Prints Division of the George Eastman House and all of the photographers who participated in our 1980 exhibition program, especially those with photographs reproduced here: Roy DeCarava, Diane Keaton, Tricia Sample, William Garnett, Edmund Teske and Dirk E. Park.

My sincere appreciation to The Friends' staff members who worked diligently on this issue: David Featherstone, Mary V. Swanson, Peter Andersen and Peggy Sexton. I would finally like to thank David Gardner and the employees of Gardner/Fulmer Lithograph for printing our efforts so beautifully.

J.A.

Picture Credits

Photographs reproduced in this book appear courtesy of the following photographers, dealers and collectors.

Cover, Grapestake Gallery, San Francisco, *page 9,* Wright Morris; *pages 11-15,* Light Gallery, New York and Los Angeles; *pages 17-21,* Robert Freidus Gallery, New York; *pages 23-27,* Mark Klett; *pages 34 & 36-40,* Harry Lunn Gallery, Washington, D.C.; *page 35,* the Gilman Paper Company Collection; *page 42,* Imogen Cunningham Trust and the International Museum of Photography at George Eastman House; *pages 43 & 44,* Stanford University Museum of Art; *page 47,* Roy DeCarava; *page 48,* James & Mary Alinder; *page 49,* William Garnett; *page 50,* Dirk E. Park; *page 51,* David Featherstone; *page 52,* Castelli Graphics, New York; *page 53,* Edmund Teske.

Untitled 25

This is the twenty-fifth in a series of publications on serious photography by The Friends of Photography. Some previous issues are still available.

ISSN 0163-7916
ISBN 0-933286-24-4
Library of Congress Catalogue Card No. 81-65401
$12.00

Cover: Richard Misrach, L.A. Series #1, 1979

Contents

Introduction

In this twenty-fifth volume of our journal, *Untitled,* we recognize and honor some important contributors to creative photography. In other articles and portfolios we present exciting discoveries in the field.

During 1980 the Trustees of The Friends of Photography approved the institution of an annual awards program. For these awards to have a greatest significance, it was decided that the selection should be made not by the Trustees or a small committee, but by a larger group of peers representing the entire field of creative photography. Thus, over the summer of 1980, a peer group of some 150 photographers, teachers, critics, curators, historians, dealers and collectors was established. No nominations were given to the peers. Instead they were presented a blank ballot on which to write their nominee for the Distinguished Career in Photography and for the Photographer of 1980. The Distinguished Career award is intended to recognize, honor and express our gratitude to a senior member of the field working on any aspect of photography. The Photographer of 1980 is intended as a mid-career award given to recognize past achievement and to encourage future work. Both awards carry a stipend of $1,000. The award recipients, Harry Callahan and Lee Friedlander, were honored in a ceremony in New York on January 20, 1981. A portfolio of their photographs and the inscriptions on their award certificates are published here as the first section of this volume.

For a decade The Friends of Photography has presented the annual Ferguson Grant to encourage the career development of a promising younger artist. Past Ferguson Grants have been awarded to Anthony Hernandez, Joseph Jachna, Ken Graves, Sally Mann, Richard Misrach, Meridel Rubenstein, Jo Ann Callis and David Maclay. The 1980 winner, Mark Klett, was selected by juror Joe Deal, a well-known photographer and Assistant Professor of Art at the University of California, Riverside. A different juror is selected each year to reflect the wide variety of concerns in current photography.

Wright Morris, the brilliant novelist, essayist and photographer, has contributed an important article, to *Untitled 25.* From the unique vantage point of a life-long involvement with both words and pictures, he cogently considers the nuances of the relationships between the two.

We are also delighted to present in this volume a portfolio of photographs by John B. Greene. Virtually unknown even today, Greene is a member of the earliest generation of photographers. He was thought until very recently to have been from the British Isles, but newly discovered information has established that he was, indeed, an American. Fewer than 200 of his photographs are known to have survived and a remarkable number of them are sure to become recognized as masterpieces of photography. In his introduction to the portfolio, the renowned historian of our medium, Beaumont Newhall, recalls not only the few known details of Greene's life but assesses the importance of his contribution.

In her informative article on the developmental years of Imogen Cunningham's photographic career, the knowledgeable and respected curator Anita Mozley clearly describes the influences which molded the technique and philosophy of this important photographer.

A portfolio selected from the 1980 exhibitions held at The Friends of Photography's gallery in Carmel is introduced by a list of the photographers who participated in our exhibition program. During the year we also organized an exhibition of Ansel Adams' landscape photographs for circulation by the United States International Communication Agency. *Ansel Adams, Photographs of the American West* will travel throughout India, North Africa and the Middle-East over the next three years. A 16-page catalogue, printed in both English and Arabic editions, was published to accompany the exhibition.

This issue ends with a list of Trustees and staff as well as the names of important contributors to The Friends of Photography. It is with this corporate and individual financial support that we are able to provide a great range of services to photography as well as offer our very inexpensive membership in the organization. We thank these donors wholeheartedly for their contributions and pledge our finest efforts in service to creative photography.

Since they are not covered elsewhere in this volume, I would like to mention here two other important program areas of The Friends: publications and workshops. During 1980 we held four major workshops. The Easter Workshop faculty included Ansel Adams, Marsha Burns, Michael Burns, Judith Golden, Richard Misrach and Olivia Parker. Our July workshop at Asilomar had as its faculty Ruth Bernhard, Jo Ann Callis, Henry Gilpin, Bill Owens and Todd Walker. Some 100 members participated in the Annual Member's Workshop and were led by a faculty of 19 instructors including Roy DeCarava, David Gardner, Wanda Hammerbeck, Pirkle Jones, John Sexton and Lou Stoumen. In October we held a special workshop for representatives of twelve non-profit photography organizations from the western United States. Another indication of The Friends' commitment to serving the field of photography, this workshop facilitated the exchange of information among the individuals who participated and the invited guest lecturers.

The publications of 1980 again showed The Friends of Photography to be a leading and innovative photography organization. Our four journal issues for the year began with *The Diana Show, Pictures Through a Plastic Lens (Untitled 21),* which explored the widespread use of an inexpensive plastic camera by creative photographers. *Images from Within, the Photographs of Edmund Teske (Untitled 22),* was a significant retrospective monograph on a remarkable and unrecognized artist. In *Nine Critics/Nine Photographs*

(Untitled 23), we asked nine critical writers in photography to discuss an important photograph about which they had strong feelings. *New Landscapes (Untitled 24),* surveyed images of the land by eight contemporary photographers and included both black and white and color portfolios.

Our major book of the year was a monograph on the art of Robert Heinecken. Through the use of photography mixed with other media, Heinecken has extended the contemporary use and meaning of the word *photography.* During the 1970s he strongly influenced the direction of photography through his teaching as well as through his work.

Untitled 25, with its stimulating articles and portfolios from the world of photography as a fine art, demonstrates the diversity of interests that can be found in the programs of The Friends of Photography. We are delighted to share *Discovery & Recognition* with you.

James Alinder
Editor
The Untitled *Series*

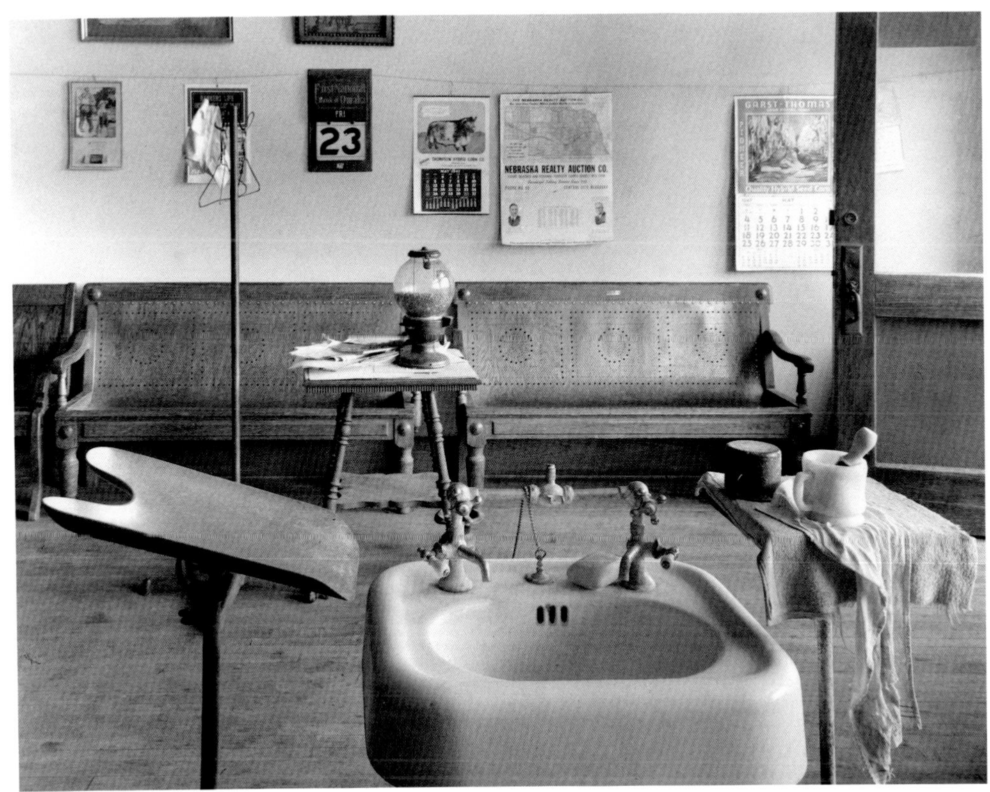

Wright Morris
Eddie Cahow's Barber Shop, Chapman, Nebraska, 1947

Harry Callahan

Distinguished Career in Photography

Elected by his peers in recognition of his career as an artist over a period of four decades, and in appreciation of his influential role as a gifted teacher of photography, this award for the Distinguished Career in Photography for 1980 is presented to Harry Callahan. Through his ingenious creativity he has enriched us with his compassionate vision. Through his selfless dedication to photography he has set a unique example for others to follow.

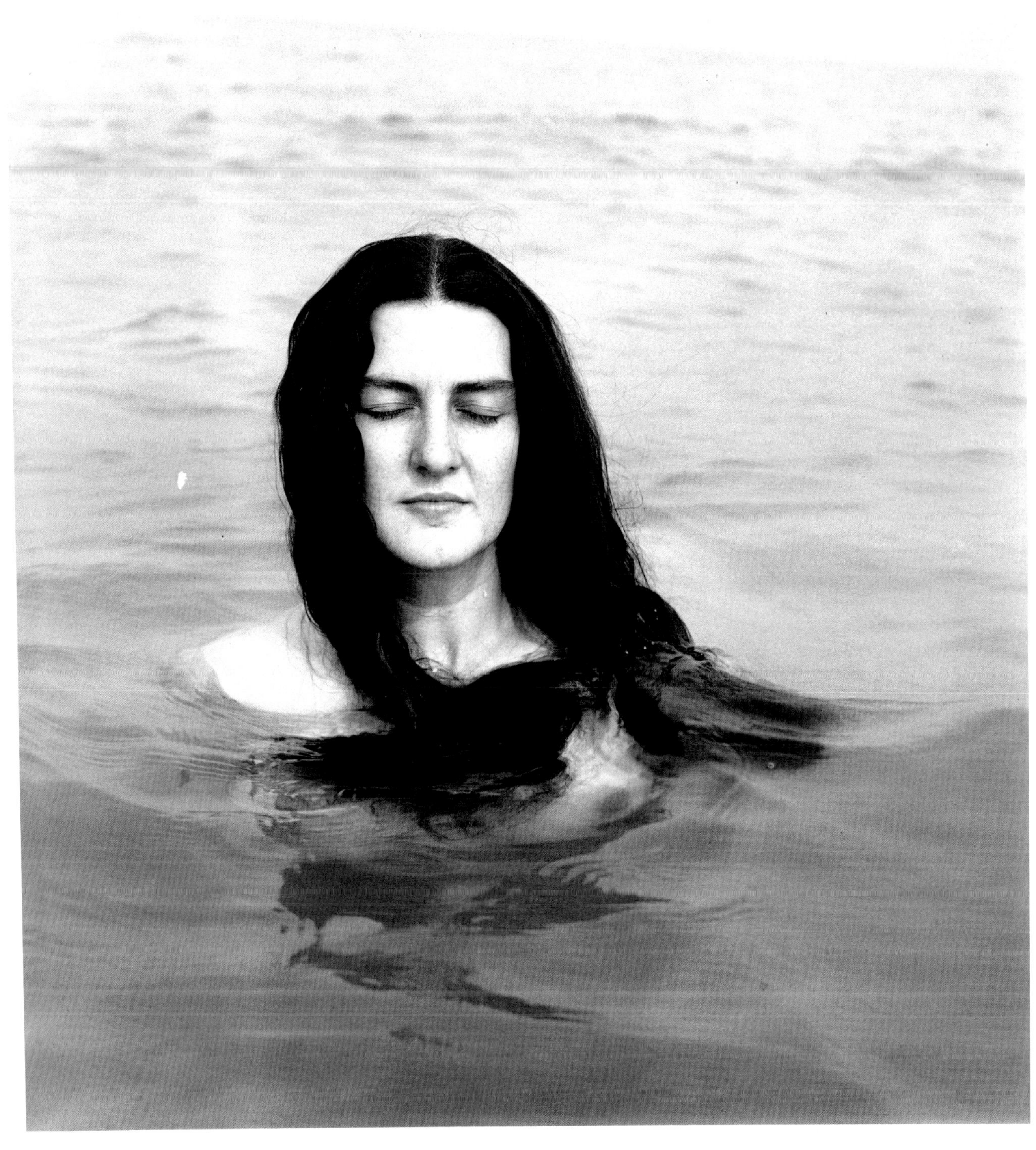

Eleanor, Chicago, 1949

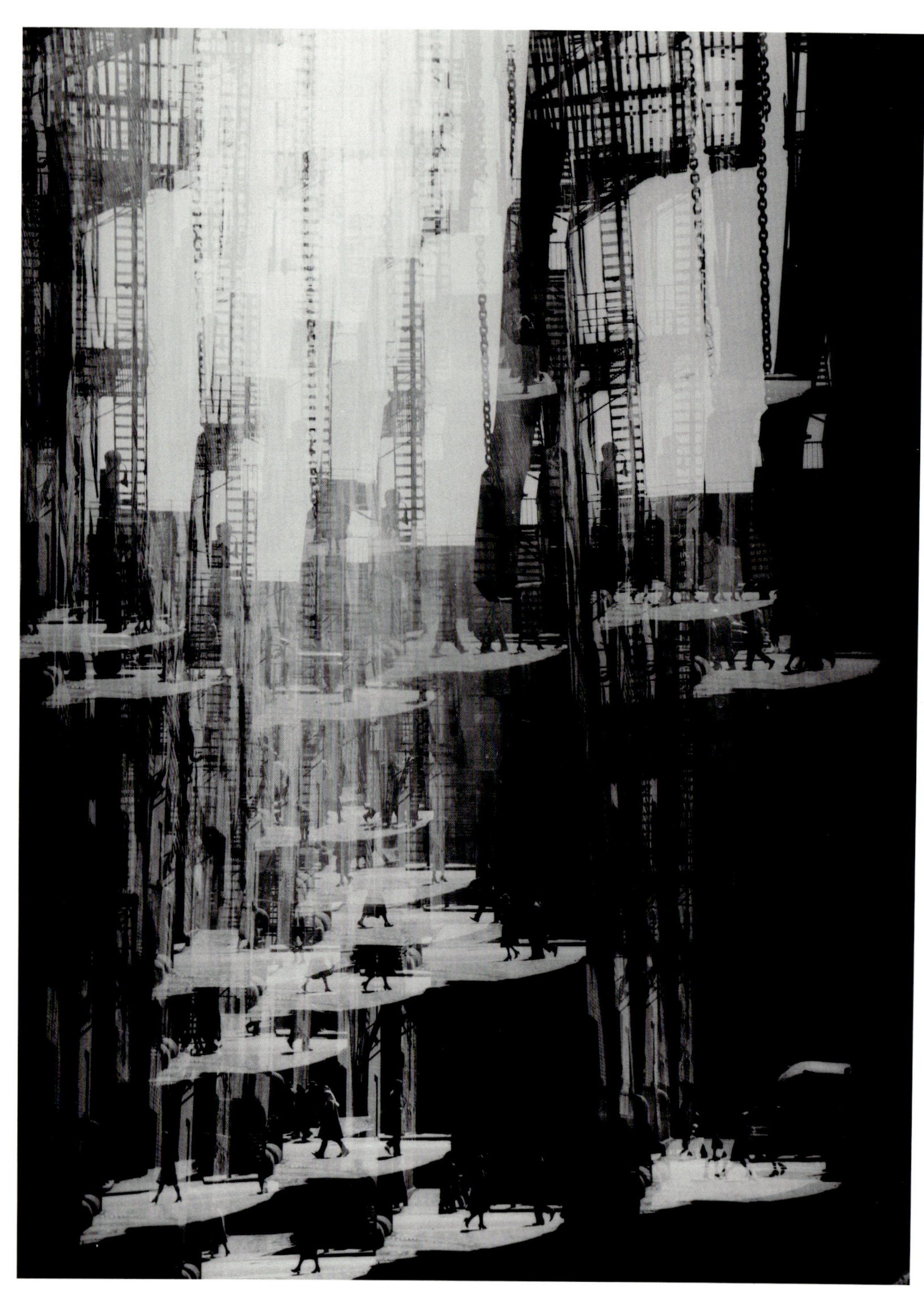

Alley, Chicago, 1948

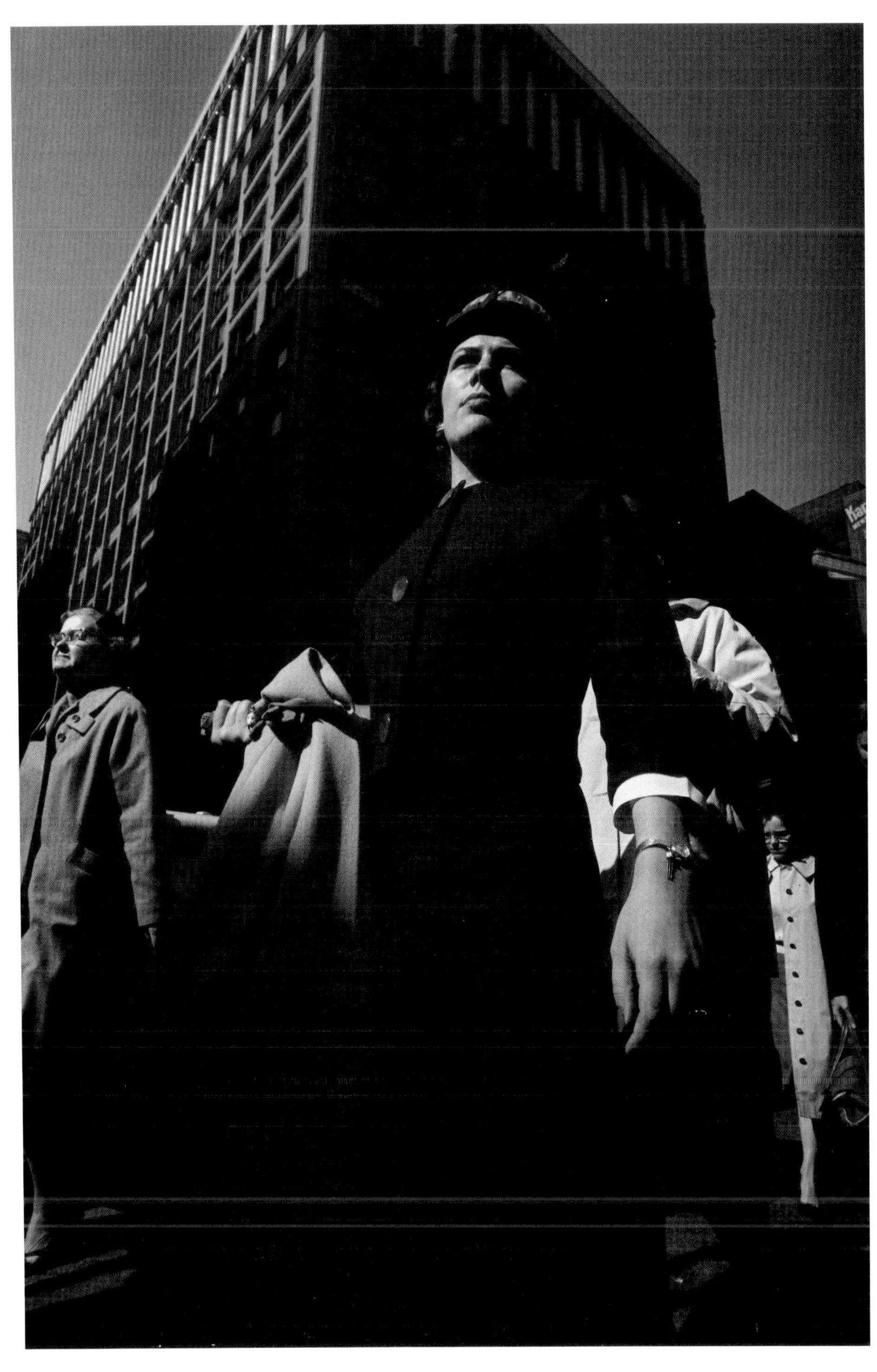

Chicago, 1961

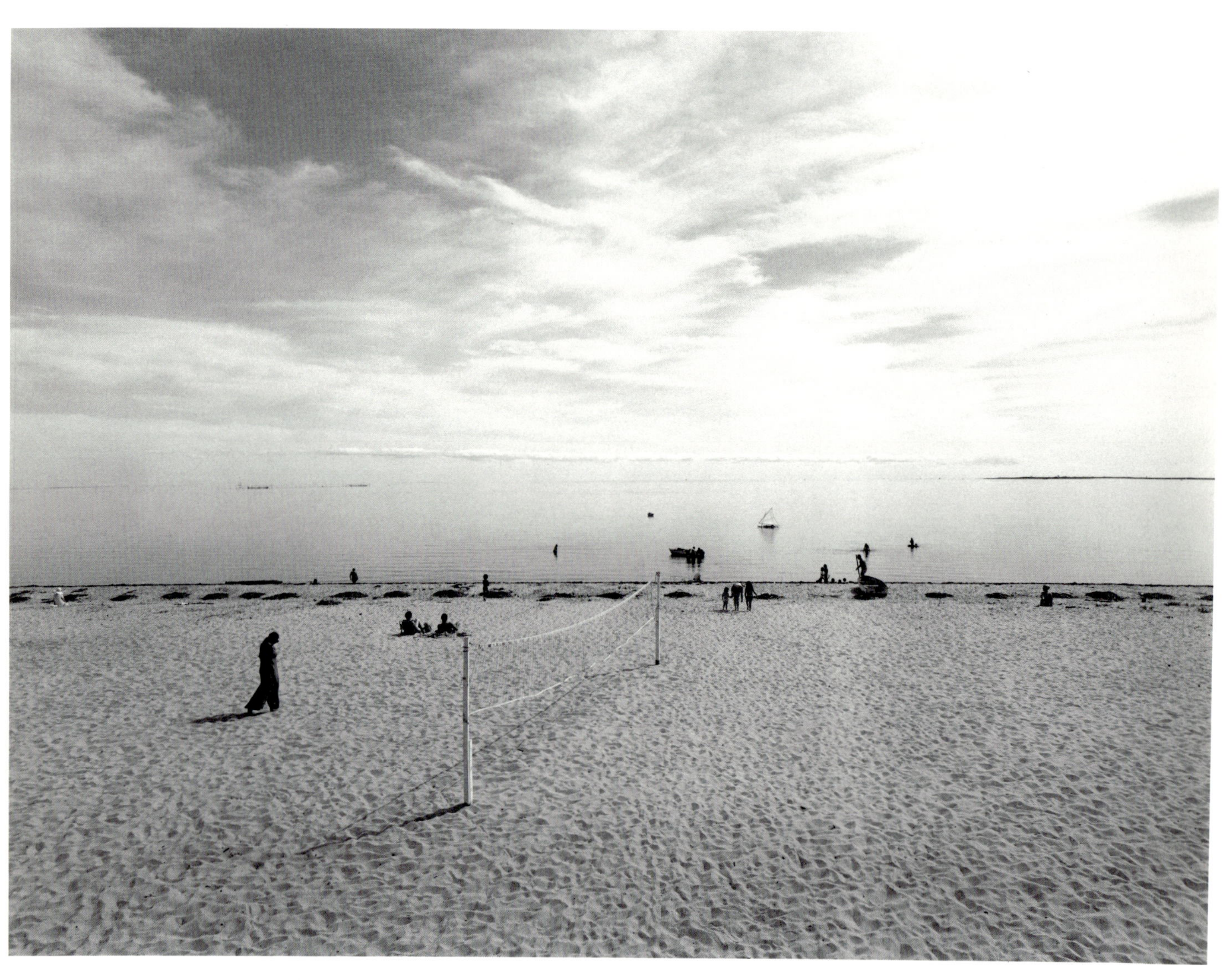

Cape Cod, 1972

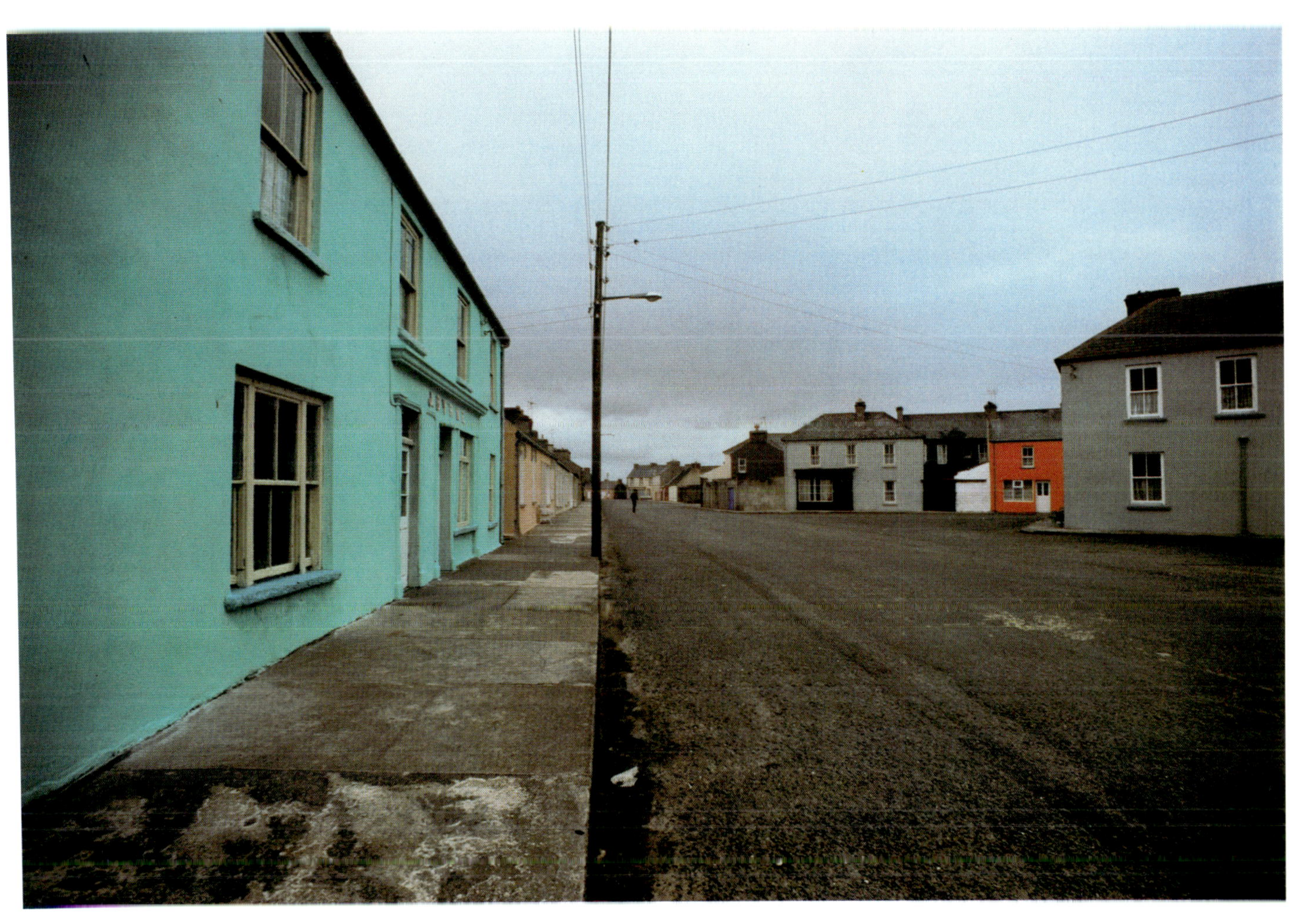

Ireland, 1979

Lee Friedlander
Photographer of 1980

Elected by his peers in recognition of his continuing contribution to photography, this award for the Photographer of 1980 is presented to Lee Friedlander. Through his precise wit and intelligence combined with a unique formalism he has influenced the content and appearance of contemporary photography. Through a prolific and significant body of work he has given us a measure by which to assess the vision of our time.

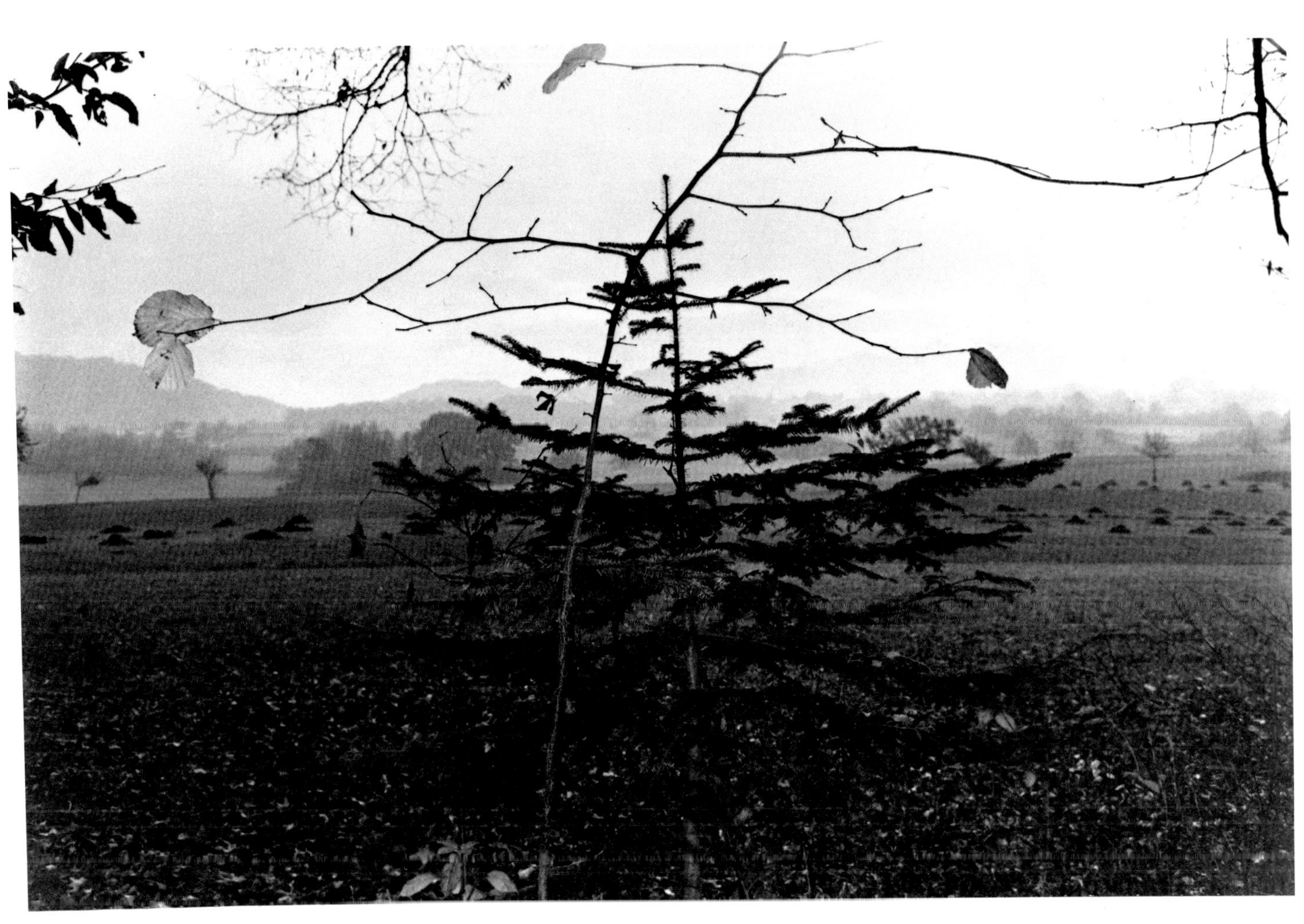

Northern France, 1972

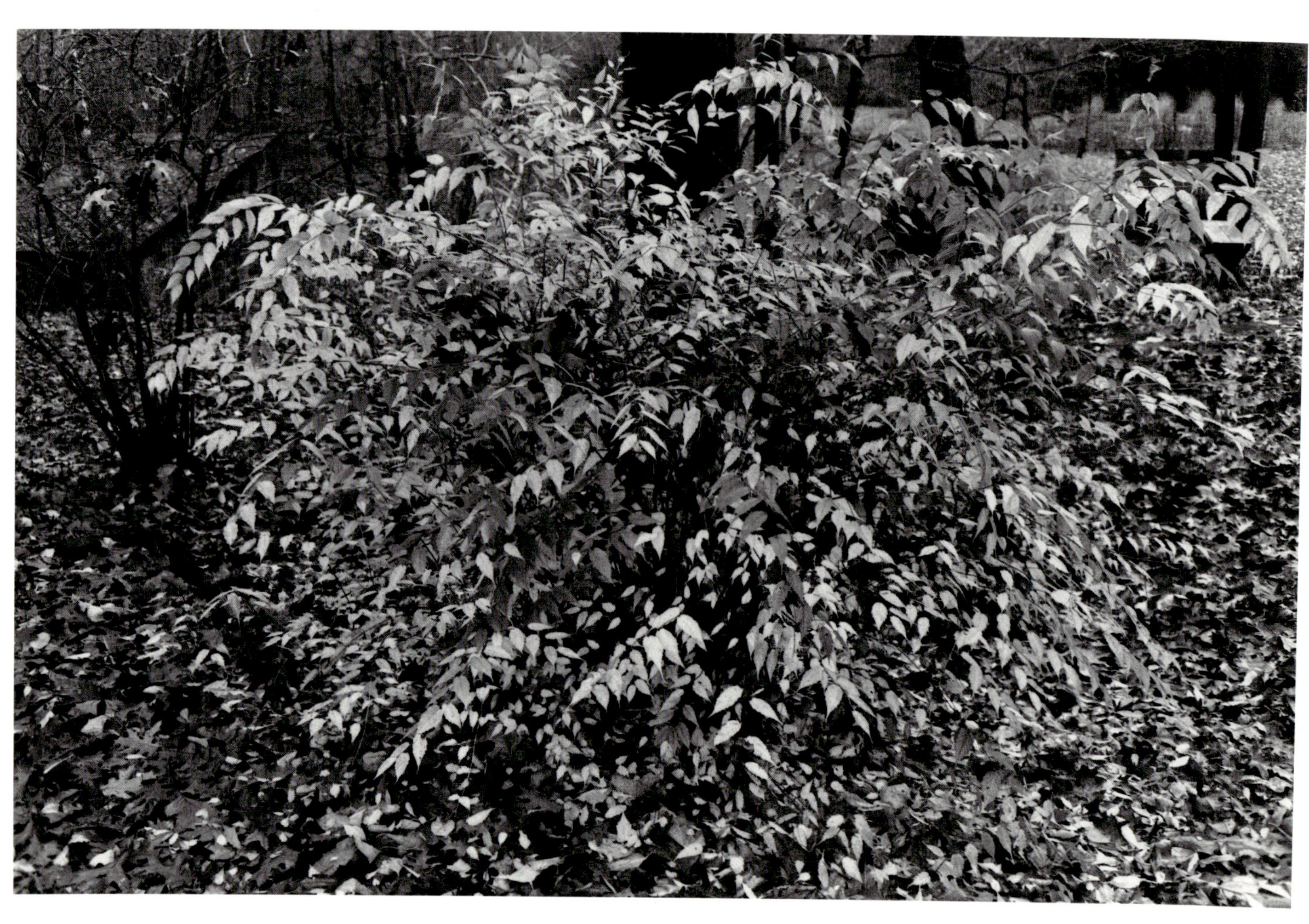

New City, New York, 1974

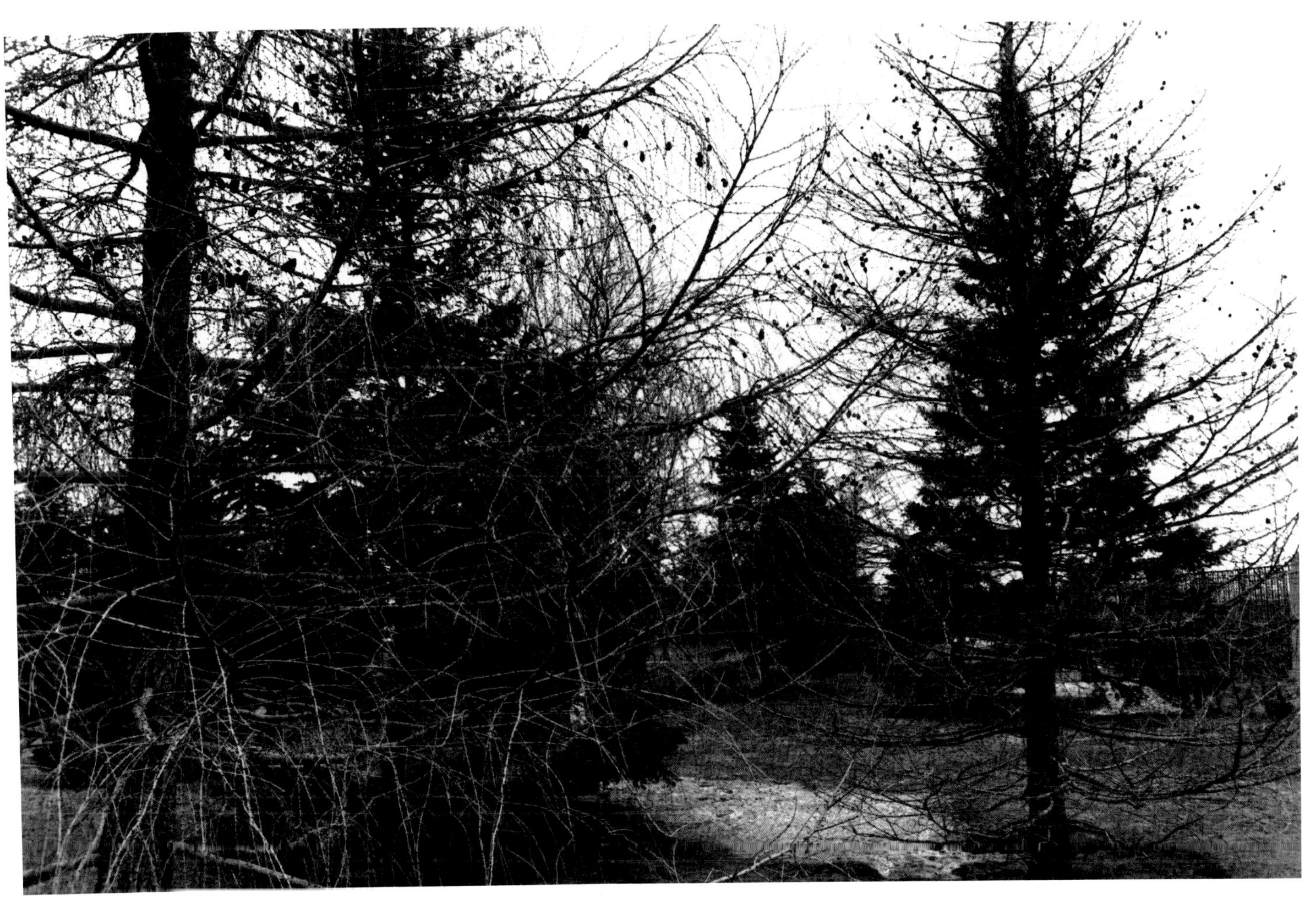

Montreal, Canada, 1975

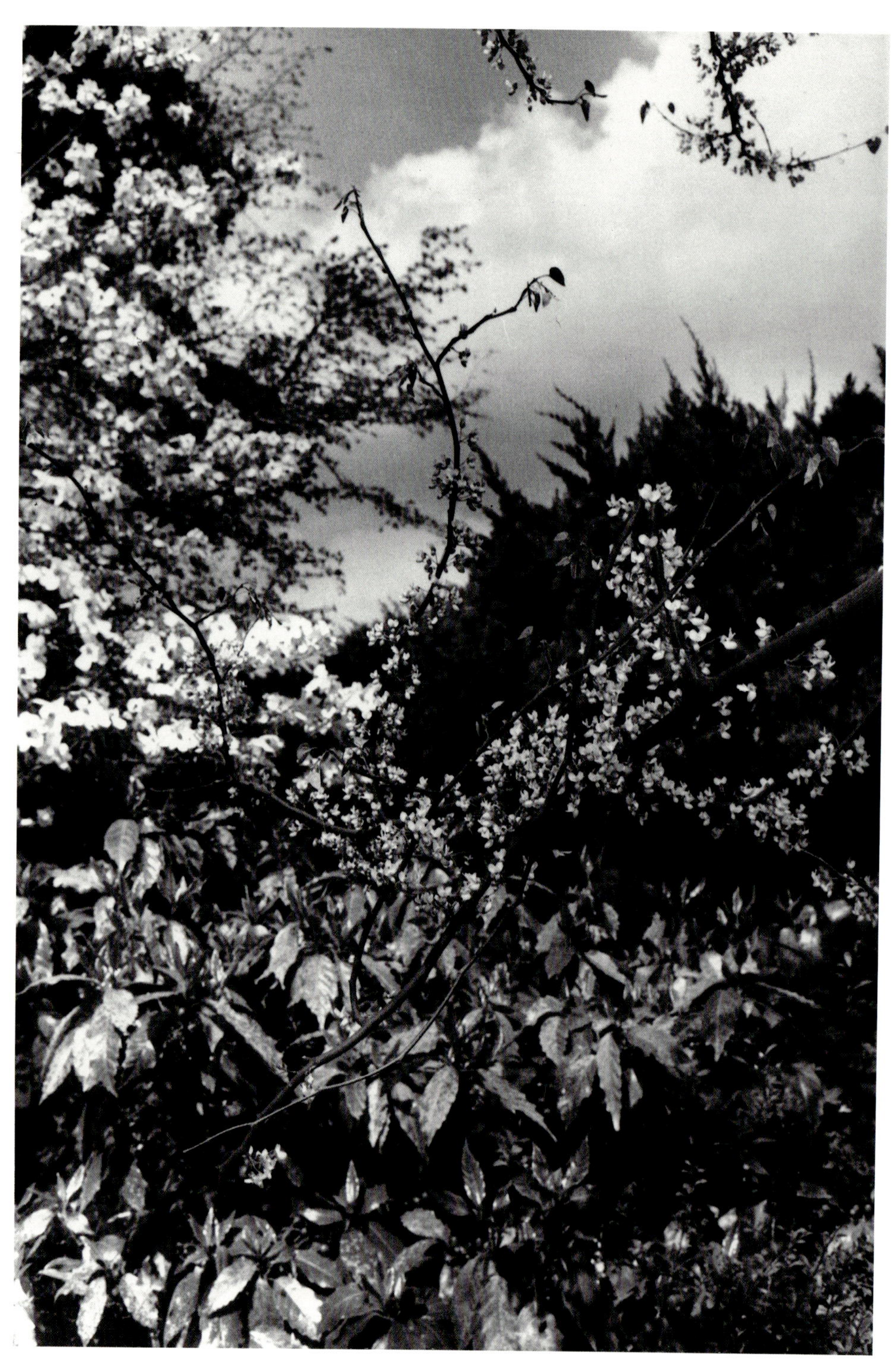

Tokyo, 1977

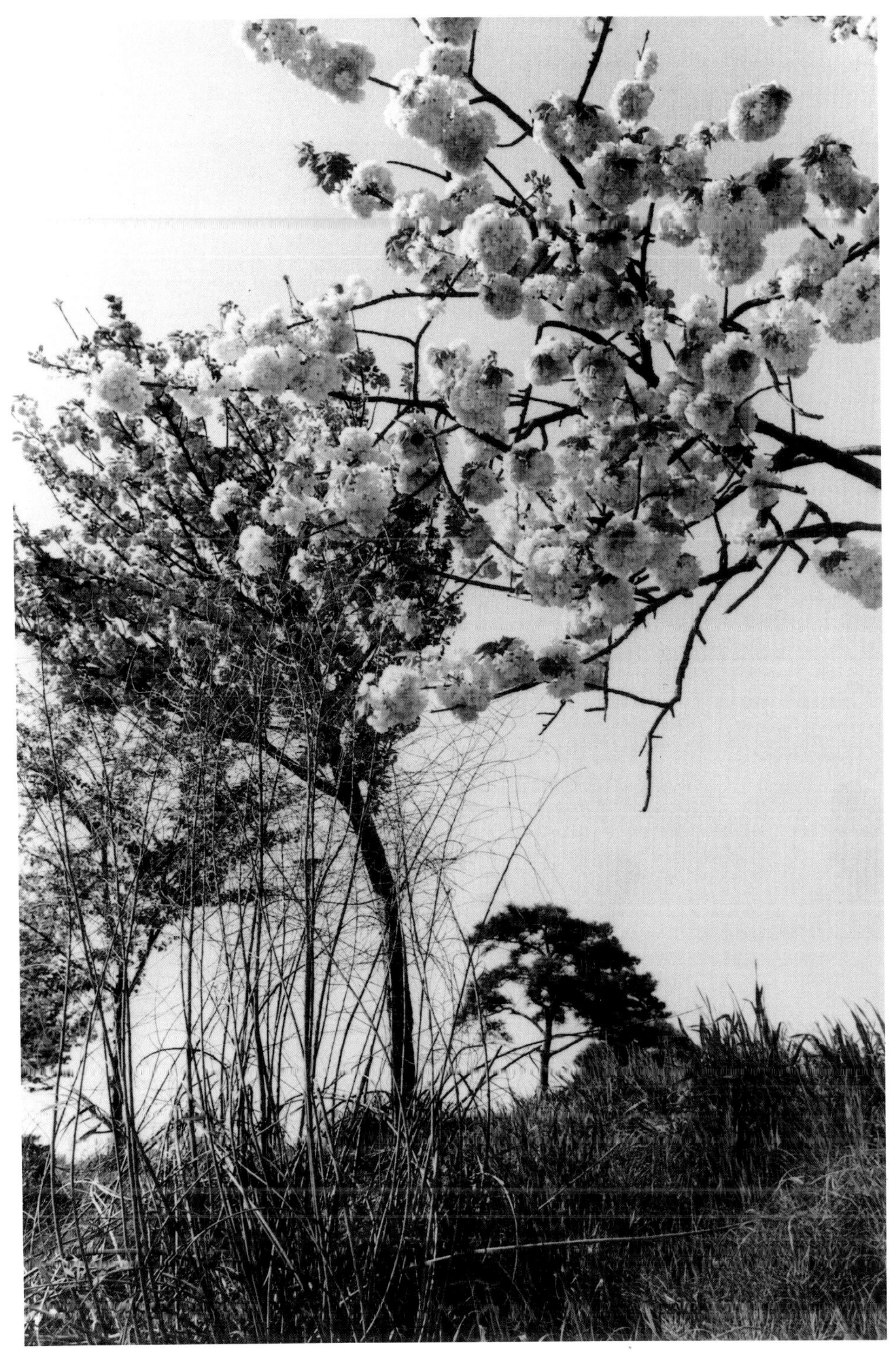

Tokyo, 1977

Mark Klett

1980 Ferguson Grant Recipient

Awarded annually by The Friends of Photography to an emerging photographer who has demonstrated excellence in and commitment to the field of creative photography, it is the purpose of the Ferguson Grant to assist in the professional and artistic growth of the recipient. A different juror is appointed to make each year's award; the selection is made on the basis of a portfolio of photographs submitted as an application.

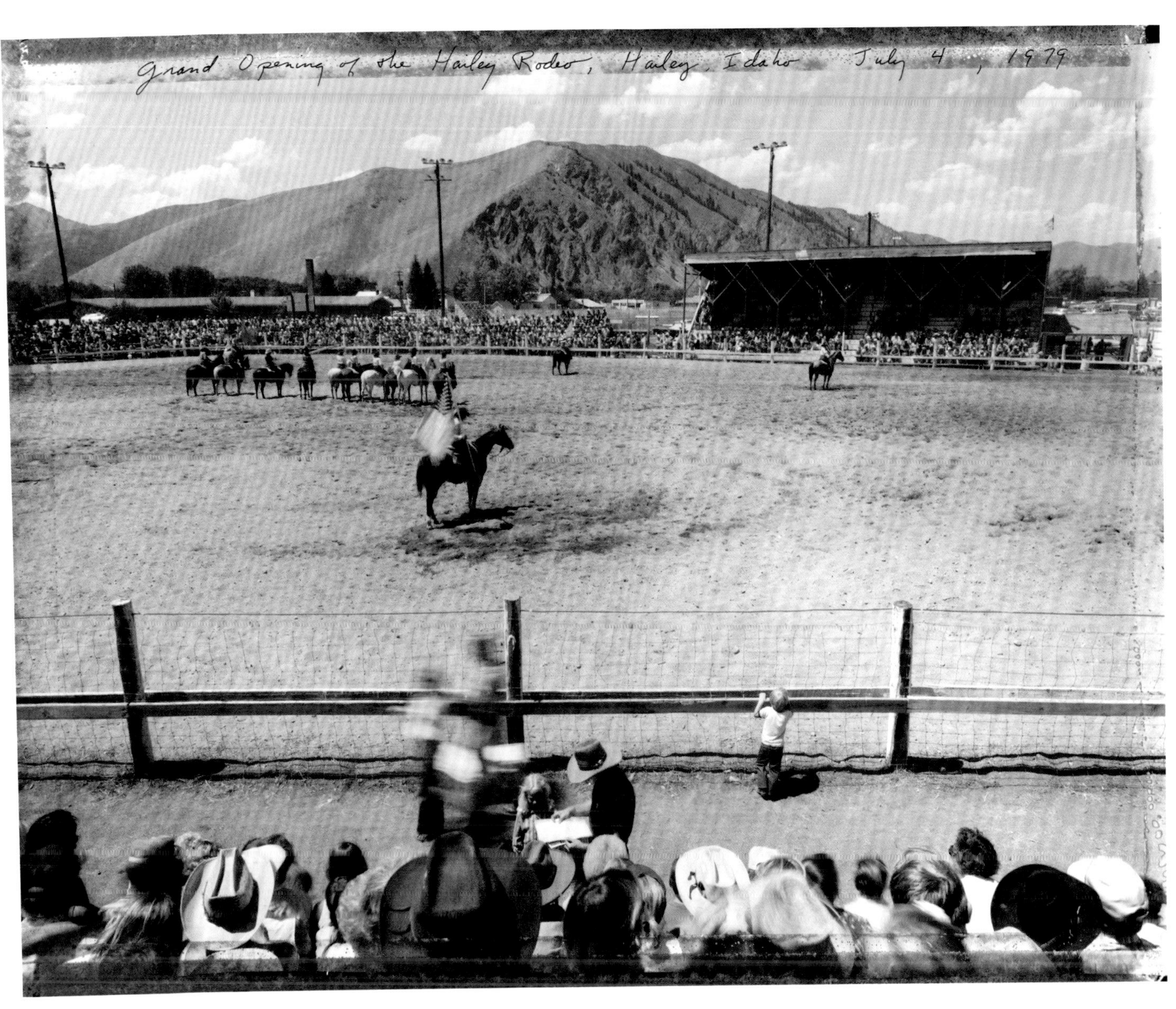

Grand Opening of the Hailey Rodeo, Hailey, Idaho, July 4, 1979.

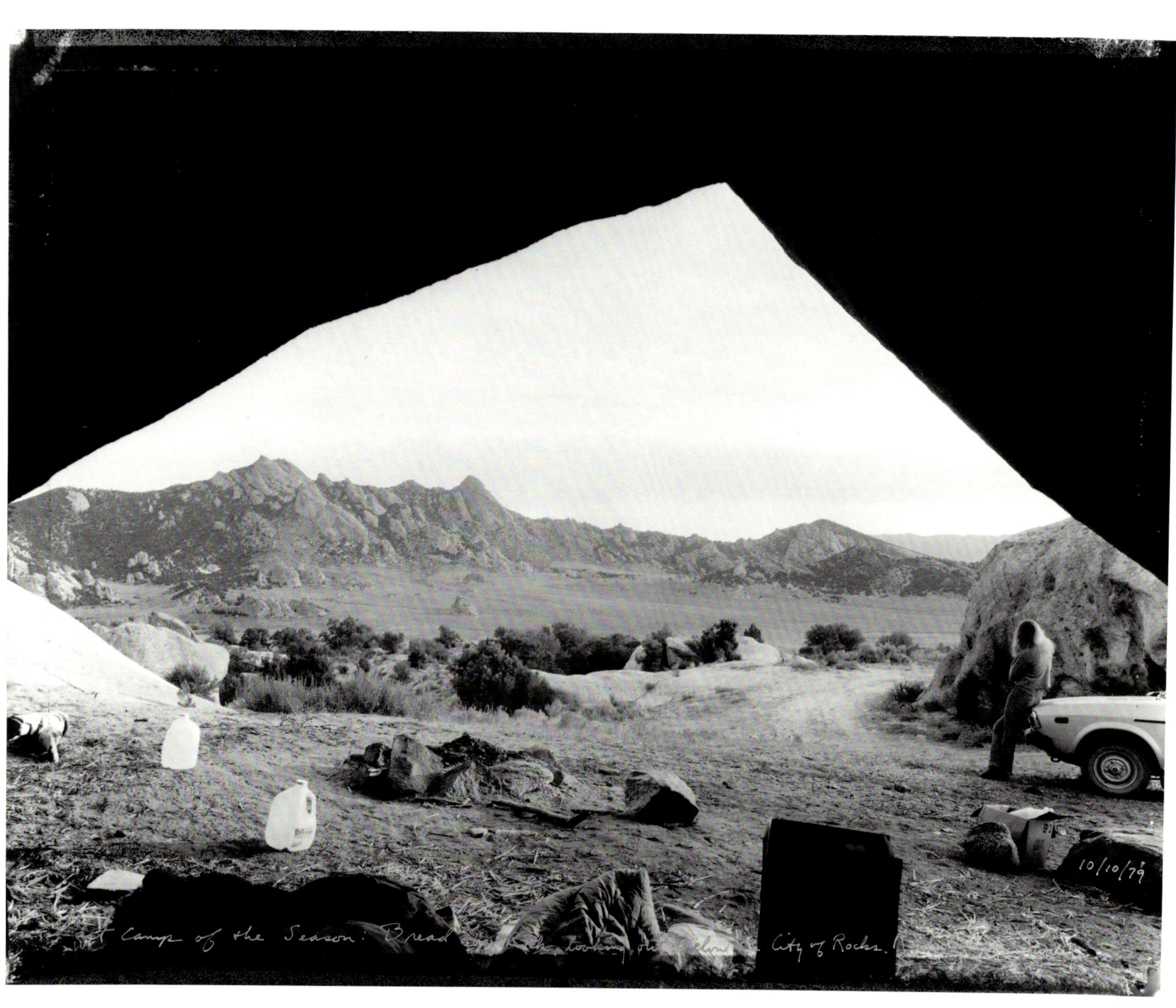

Last Camp of the Season: Bread Loaf Rock, Looking Out, Below the City of Rocks. Rephotographic Survey, 10/10/79.

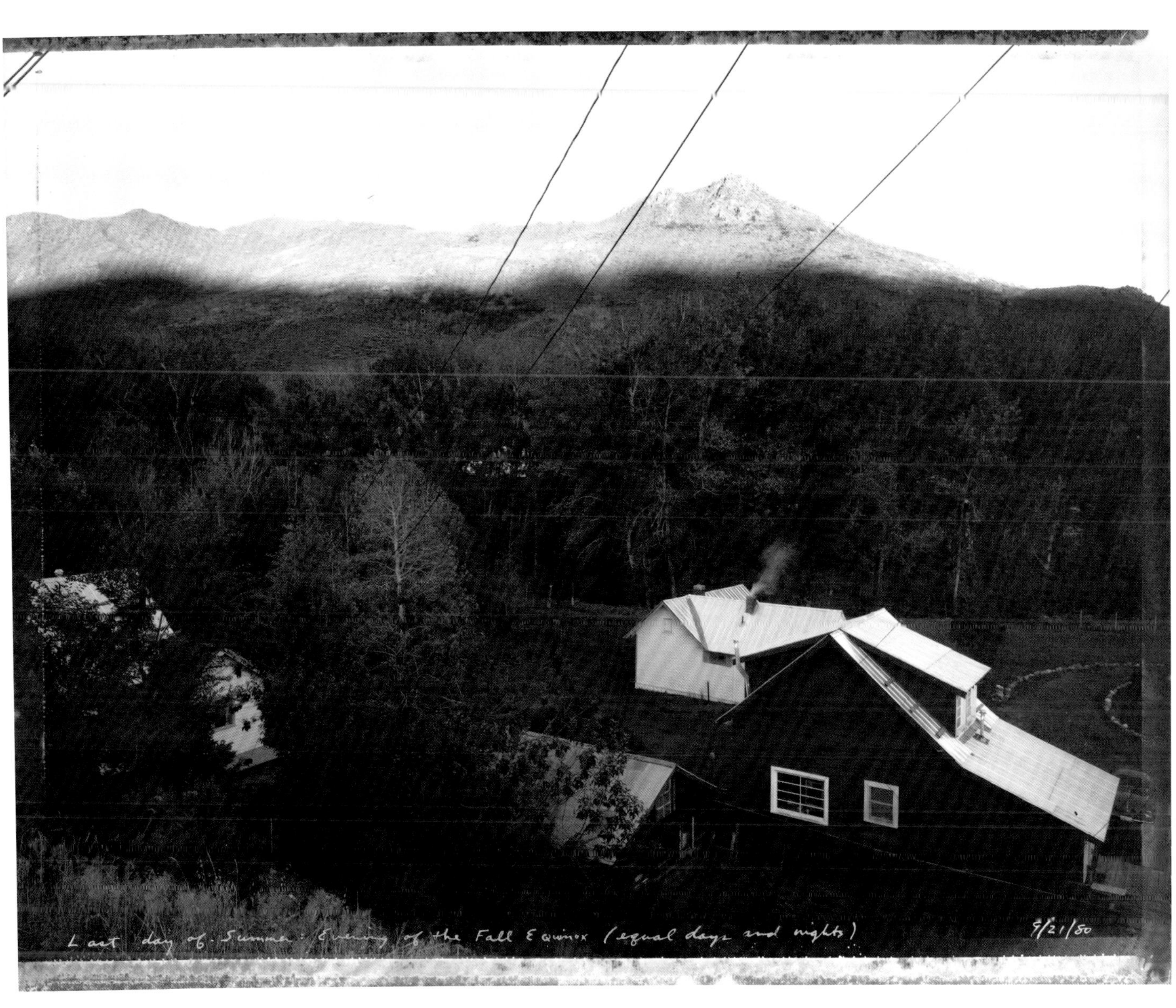

Last Day of Summer: Evening of the Fall Equinox (Equal Days and Nights). 9/21/80.

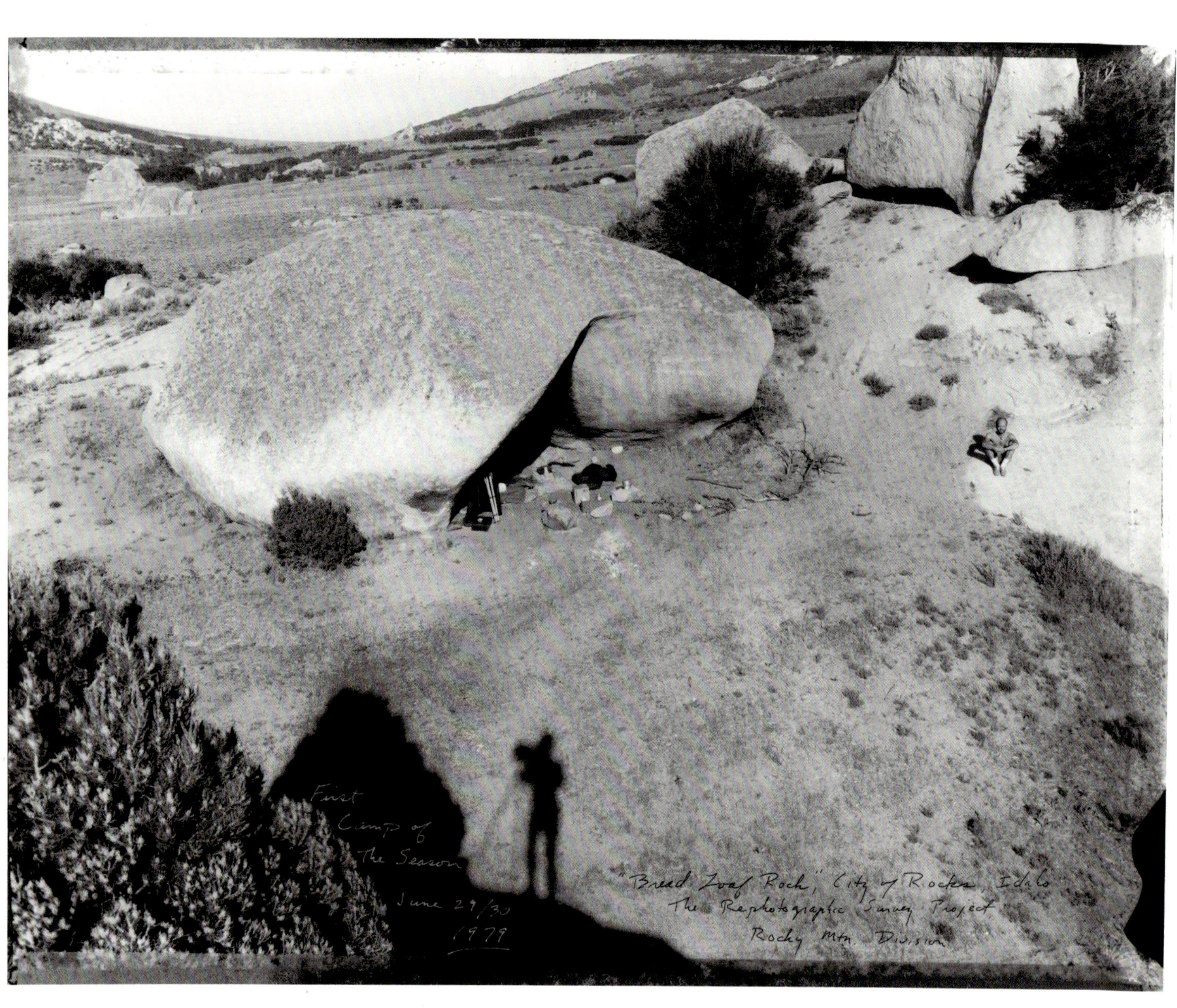

First Camp of the Season: Bread Loaf Rock, City of Rocks, Idaho, June 29/30, 1979.

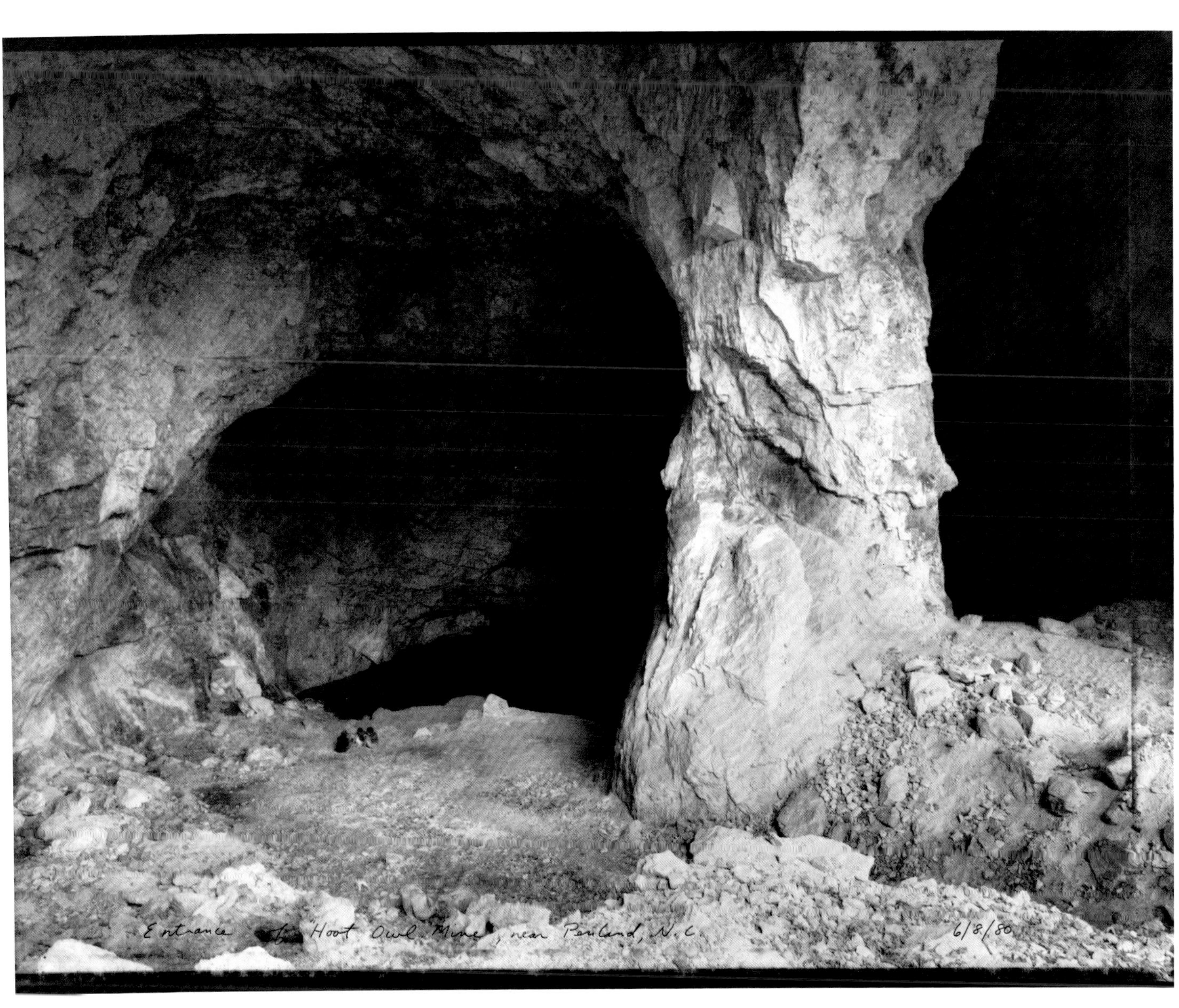

Entrance of Hoot Owl Mine, near Penland, North Carolina, 6/8/80

Photographs, Images and Words

Wright Morris

In 1889, in Custer County, Nebraska, a pioneer who had failed at farming had the time to ponder the brave new world around him. What he saw cried for confirmation. In this treeless landscape, blazing with light, a frozen waste over the winter, baked by the sun in the summer, the inhabitants took refuge in sod houses, as other creatures burrowed into holes. These circumstances bred a new breed of people, and made of the pioneer a photographer. Solomon Butcher was one of the first specialists. On the frontier, taste had not yet decreed nor practice established what was appropriate as a photographic subject. Time was also needed, and much tactful persuasion, to lure these cave dwellers into the open. *Why* they were there would never be visible in the photographs. This overriding question, the first to be asked by those living elsewhere, was of profound interest to Butcher but not one that he found puzzling. Being one of them he knew its answer, and this knowledge led them to trust him. We call them pioneers, a native breed of visionaries.

This vision is not self-evident in the photographs. We catch glimpses of it in the objects Butcher persuaded some of them to bring from their soddies, their treasured possessions assembled in the manner of a family portrait. A chair with cushions, a bird in its cage, a sewing machine, a Christmas wreath like a branch of the Golden Bough, an elegant foot-pedaled organ, with glistening keys, the music open on the rack, around which the family is gathered. One child will be in the mother's arms, another on the father's knee. In the middle ground, between them and the soddy, perhaps a few cows or pigs, or the team hitched to a wagon, or a valued piece of farm machinery, all set off against the dark mound of the soddy, the black hole of the doorway, the grass on the roof blending with the sea of grass that surrounds it. About this "image" there is nothing candid. It is as posed and considered as a studio portrait.

The inhabitants have come from the house to stand in the pitiless glare of the light. The man is hatless. His face has been blackened by the wind and sun but his forehead gleams as if scalped. He wears a collarless, clean white shirt; his wife a seldom worn Sunday dress. It was not lost on Butcher that these portraits have the quality of icons. In many details they resemble creches appropriate to a Holy Family. On this frontier all possessions are life enhancing and have their place. The photographer wanted everything in the picture but himself. He had by nature the "photographer's eye", but he did not have his ego. We see in Butcher's work how the eye can function as an invisible part of the image.

Possessed by a similar obsession to record what he saw around him, Eugene Atget had begun to photograph the city of Paris. Both photographers used the camera to confirm what was visible. Each was a part of the life he photographed. In their practice we have examples that clarify some, if not all, current photographic dilemmas — such as what should come first, the photograph or the photographer.

These sod-house inhabitants, with their gaze on the future, did not see themselves as the camera saw them. They did not smile or mug. They did not wave to the man behind it. For them it was a moment of stopped time in a fevered dream. Can we say that the photographer's "eye" has its origin in this complex awareness of time? A piece of it is captured, but in the blurred image we see that it continues. An awareness of this gives every photograph its poignancy.

Let us imagine a photographers' tour making a field trip to the plains of Nebraska. We will choose a point in time in which we see it flowing in both directions. Nadar will be there, with his portable darkroom, and Diane Arbus with her small camera. I would also like Stieglitz to be there, and Edward Weston, as well as Dorothea Lange and Walker Evans, Cecil Beaton and Richard Avedon. They are all met and led by Butcher to a sod house in Custer County, a piece of time in situ. A pioneer and his wife, with their shoeless children and what they have in the way of possessions, are assembled to be "shot" in the yard at the front. Just to one side, but sharing equal billing, is a team of white horses in black harness, hitched to a topless buggy. The sun shines. The light glares. A breeze stirs the grass on the soddy roof. In some of the photographs this grass will appear as a blur. At a signal from Butcher all the photographers begin to work.

Can we say there is something here for everyone? Time itself will prove to be more of a problem than the subject. Nadar is already at work on the archetypal portrait of the American gothic. The pioneer holds a pitchfork. His wife is reluctant to remove the bonnet that shades her face. Weston has turned from the subject to the sea of grass that waves in patterns of light and shade to the horizon. Lange and Evans are at ease with material they have mastered. While waiting for his turn to photograph the woman, Stieglitz contemplates the cloud formations. Cecil Beaton has begun an "arrangement" of the unusual artifacts available while Avedon prepares a backdrop for a few clinical close-ups. The clicking sound that we hear is the camera of Diane Arbus, seated in the buggy, from where she takes candid snaps of the photographers at work. Only Bellocq — if he had come along — would not have troubled to unpack his equipment, looking forward eagerly to Dodge City, Kansas, next stop on the tour.

Among these diverse and contrasting points of view, the intrinsically unifying element is not the subject but the medium. They are all photographers. What they are taking are photographs. Some seek confirmation, some self-expression, some documentation, a few have in mind revelation; but so long as they use the camera, what they are taking are photographs. On these discordant impressions of the same subject, time will confer a touch of the miraculous.

In 1900, in Manchester, England, on the day the first electric train service was inaugurated, a photograph was taken to commemmorate the event. At the center of the picture, high on its tripod, is a camera, with the photographer standing on a box behind it. Since he is not the one who took the picture his presence *within* the picture indicates its importance. On the left are the trams festooned with garlands of flowers; a policeman, with two citizens, walks from the picture toward a troublemaker. On the right, densely packed, is a motley assembly of citizens. The day is sunless. There is industrial smog in the air of the new century. The eyes of the crowd are turned from the scene itself to look toward the photographer outside the picture. A boy in his early teens, a cap cocked on his head, grips his lapels, thrusting his chest forward like a politician at the word of victory. His glance toward the camera is at once assured and self-appraising. Fame has touched him. Unmistakably he says, "Here I am!"

This is but one of numberless thousands of *anonymous* photographs that give us a magical glimpse into the past, a fragment snipped from the film of time. A more sophisticated, self-aware photographer would have been more selective, found a less conventional point of view and given us his own impression of the event. This might have heightened its drama, its "human" interest, at the expense of what we now feel to be authentic — life mirrored not by ourselves but by life itself.

Impressions dominate our myriad responses, testifying infallibly to our presence, but intrinsic to the photograph is an aura of detachment. However much the artist may feign it, only the photograph, by its nature, is it. We see it most clearly in that genre of photographs we have referred to as anonymous. Cameras took them. In that lies their authenticity. The lad preening himself in the right-hand corner may or may not have caught the eye of the photographer — he catches ours.

"All the arts," André Bazin wrote, in a statement I consider inexhaustibly ponderable, "are based on the presence of man, only photography derives an advantage from his absence." The camera takes the pictures. The photographer is empowered to enhance or diminish what the camera takes.

Custom has staled our awareness that the photograph is Magic. We see it but we do not grasp it. It is as commonplace and as mystifying as sight. The first men to intuit its miraculous powers worked in secret, like alchemists, and kept their records in code. In 1832 Nicéphore Niepce, long pregnant with he knew not what, applied himself to giving the unknown an appropriate name. He did this in the hope that it would make familiar what was passing strange, and prove to be an act of possession.

1. Painting by nature herself
2. Copy by nature herself
3. Portrait by nature herself
4. To show nature herself
5. Real nature
6. True copy of nature

His instincts were that whatever it was, it was a *piece* of nature. In this list there is no mention of Niepce as the prime mover, or the creator. It is nature herself he wants to acknowledge. In the fullness of time (as might have been predicted) the camera holder will prove to be less awestruck. Instead of a portrait or a painting by nature *herself,* it will be by the photographer. He will see himself not merely as the picture taker, but increasingly as the picture maker. The results of this deliberate appropriation, as we see it in the photo-secessionist movement, is a notable gain in pictorial interest at the expense of photographic authenticity — that is to say, at the expense of the photograph.

This amounts to a welcome gain at the expense of an irreplaceable loss. Photographers were quick to recognize this imbalance and set about recouping the losses. The collaboration desired, and achieved, is what is modern in modern photography but present and at ease in much that is old. The recognition of this quality we have enshrined with the word "image". It was not one of the words Nicéphore Niepce had in mind, nor was it in the mind of his generation, being a perceptive and innovative way to relate the picture, the picture maker and the subject.

"Images" result if the presence of the photographer is felt to be an enhancement of the photograph. The portraits of Cameron, the "decisive moments" of Lartigue, Atget's views of Paris, share this apparent enhancement. It may be present through deliberate artistic intent, as in Cameron, or through a precocious talent, as in Lartigue, or through long receptivity and appropriation, as in the example of Atget. The absence of the photographer, in the anonymous photograph, often contributes to our impression of the print as an image. We acknowledge the result to be an original object. The recognition of this *image,* now a commonplace, makes an essential, rather than an incidental, distinction between many photographs possible. This photo-image claims, with other man-made artifacts, a self-sufficient uniqueness. Rather than a likeness, it has become a thing itself.

Although the image's presence can be appreciated, it should not be formulated, since in the photograph *time,* even more than taste, influences our impressions and colors our judgments. The explicitly documentary photograph makes the best, and the most, of its warring elements and its reluctance to be judged as a "picture." This conflict between the pictorial and the documentary gives many photographs a dramatic tension that seeks resolution in a "decisive moment." A residue of unresolved elements will often heighten, rather than weaken, the resulting image. The photographs by Van Schaick, Hine, Riis, Evans, Lange and numberless others are unavoidably more than social comments, and provide us with more than a message. Pictorial elements — we might say happily — both corrupt and enhance the most searing social statement. There is a remnant of the *image* in every documentary, and the leavings of the document in every image. These inherent contradictions distinguish the photograph and need not be resolved.

The camera image differs from all others in the way it resists isolation. The word "bleed," used to describe a photograph printed or mounted without margins, accurately conveys the cutting off, the excision, the amputation, of the photograph from its environment. The habit of "framing" pictures accustoms us to what is visually bizarre. *Where* is what is missing? In what mysterious way does it relate to what has been captured? The controlled conditions of studio portraits — the false environment of props and lighting — avoid the hard, bleeding edges and give the illusion of wholeness. There are no severed connections. Within the frame, as W.H.F. Talbot was the first to remark, there is often much that will prove to be new as the photographer ponders what he has done. It is not unusual for a photograph to be inexhaustible.

"At the thought of the eye," Darwin said, "I grow cold all over." And some frisson of this chill — like the motions of plants underwater — should pass along the nerves of those who take, make and look at photographs. Anything so miraculous is compelled to become commonplace.

This rise in what is perceived, which is a rise in status, has its price. As an image, the photograph is defanged, in a way denatured, and made accessible to art. Photographs that are brutal, obscene or merely disgusting can be exhibited as images. No one has yet (to my knowledge) mounted an exhibition of the photographs of Belsen and Dachau, but our remarkable appetite for visual sensations makes it not only possible but inevitable. If the option is open, someone will take it.

As a girl of twelve, Susan Sontag first set eyes on the photographs of Dachau. She speaks of this occasion as one that divided her life into two parts: before this exposure and after. There is no confusion in her mind, or in ours, that she saw photographs, not images. She goes on to observe that to suffer is one thing but to live with photographic images of suffering can be a corrupting experience. It is the "image" that makes this possible, even fashionable. Avedon's dying father challenges the observer to justify his own participation in his dying. The observer's shudder of over-exposure attests to the photographs' validity, as well as to his own distressed and embarrassed humanity. Quantities of male and female flesh now attest to the current clichés of liberation. If we feel shame, embarrassment or disgust, we have the assurance that the image has not obliterated the photograph.

A commercial photographer I know has been taking pictures for more than half a century, ever since he was given his first Brownie. Among the thousands of prints, the tens of thousands of negatives, are the jumbled contents of our life and times. If all others were lost, this archive might well serve as our portrait. But only on rare occasions do these pictures bring to mind the man who took them. There are babies, kittens, old and wrecked cars; proud parents, glowing brides (flesh tones have been heightened, teeth whitened); summer outings, forest murmurs; oversize and undersize vegetables, eggs and fruit; construction sites, burned and razed buildings, streets and houses, real estate offerings; locomotives, cabooses; pliers, wrenches and gadgets; hippie weddings, prominent divorces, famous and infamous people; and the war in Korea while he did his stint in the Army. In the context of the new and the ultramodern, some of these photographs are new as tomorrow. The shifting sands of fashion and taste have finally caught up with what he has been doing all his life. But there is no need to mention his name since he is not a "name" photographer.

My friend's passport photos sell for four dollars. Fancy portraits in a frame cost more. Cats like him. He is good with pets and children. If something is visible he will take a picture of it. The secret ingredient in all his photographs is time. The passage of time will confer on his archive much that now seems to be lacking. "Look at that!" they will say, whereas now they just look.

I thought of him some months ago when I came on the news that a photograph by Ansel Adams was offered for sale for tens of thousands of dollars. One of a kind, perhaps? Or one of a kind in the hands of a dealer? Considered as Art, photographs are now subject to the fads and practices of the art market. An artificially created rarity is used to sustain or inflate market prices. The dealer who acquires a photographer's negatives is free to control or exploit this market. Since anyone can, and millions do, buy cameras and take pictures, the oversupply will always exceed the market's demand. Although photographic discussion might continue to be fevered, the buying, selling and speculation in photographs must confine itself to a sampling of what is offered. It is time — before it is talent — that confers interest

and significance on the photograph, and time cannot be speeded up to the dealer's advantage. If it were sufficiently profitable, most photographers could take or duplicate many photographs. In *Edward Weston: Fifty Years,* his wife Charis Weston wrote:

> The Guggenheim trips were like elaborate treasure hunts, with false clues among the genuine ones. We were always being directed by friends to their own favorite sights, views or formations . . . (Weston) knew my eyes were at his service, and that the moment anything with a "Weston" look appeared, I would stop the car and wake him up.

Today there would be little need to wake him. The recognition of a Weston picture could be followed by its taking. If Weston-type photographs prove to be profitable, and the expanding market will absorb them, photographers with the skill to take them will not be hard to find. What the camera and the chemicals have done for one photographer they will also do for another. It is a bit early to open this Pandora's box, but it is there and waits on the occasion.

As of the moment the uses of photography, not to mention the abuses, defy the efforts of critics and scholars to make sensible distinctions. Among the Yoruba of western Nigeria portrait photography of considerable interest has been integrated into the culture. It had its origin in English colonial examples, but it thrives on, meeting immediate cultural needs. Stephen Sprague, an American photographer, found ten flourishing photographic studios in a town without electricity or running water — facilities important to photographers. Each of the studios featured scenic props that provided an environment for the sitter and often constituted, in their originality, a piece of constructivist art. To operate his enlarger, one photographer ingeniously employed the headlight of his motorcycle, with the motor running, to provide a source of light. The most striking of these Yoruba portraits, giving the photographs uniqueness, are the portraits of twins, one of whom had died. In this extremity a second photograph of the living twin was substituted, the two images placed side by side. A conscious and skillful effort was made to remove the evidence that they were actually two separate pictures.

In these Yoruba portraits the non-native observer is confronted with images of a complexity and sophistication far beyond the intent of the photographer. How are the mandarin tastes of a few collectors to be applied to the practice of the Yoruba, not to mention examples still to be discovered? It seems inevitable that these unique, one-of-a-kind portraits will find their way to the expanding photographic market. Rarity will be ensured, until it gets around that they bring a price.

To accommodate the growing number of artists and the multifarious activities now loosely described as art, distinctions necessary to intelligent discussion have been obliterated. In the vast accumulation of conflicting opinion there is one unifying element: all of it is in words. The art work no longer speaks for itself. It is ironic to think, as the words flow, that the photograph was once thought to speak a more concrete, less abstract language. The slogan was that it was better than a thousand words. Thousands upon thousands of words now encumber a quantity of photographs. This flowering of writing about photography, much of it readable, informative and innovative, is the latest example of the current cultural mania to transform one thing into another, and eventually into words. To *reside* in one thing or another appears to be impossible. On the evidence the thing itself — the person, the object, the painting, the book, the music, the sunset, the operation — exists primarily as a point of departure, a launching pad from which we take off into an orbit of our own. The more controversial art becomes and the more heat it generates, the more words it requires. These deflections from the things themselves comprehend most of what we call culture. Book reviews, art reviews, movie reviews, sports reviews feed a greater and more ponderable need than does the book, the work of art, the movie or the sporting event. Greater than our hunger for sensation is the need we feel to know of what it consists. We have read the book, attended the exhibit, seen the movie and so on, but what they consist of are the images that have been put into words. Photographs, photographs of all things, were once believed to offer a point of resolution. They offered a stop in the flow of time as well as in the endless stream of our responses. The observer looked. The photograph soberly returned his gaze.

All criticism is in the process of becoming a new genre of fiction, as fiction itself seems to be threatened. The overgrazed world of experience, appropriate to the novel, can be reappraised and reexperienced as criticism. In the same way, the overgrazed world of visible artifacts and events can be recreated as verbal images.

In this practice the recognition of some photographs as "works of art" is less an infiltration of art by photography than an appropriation, on the part of art, of photographic authenticity. We see this in current art enthusiasms. Momentarily the abstract is exhausted. Every effort is made to incorporate the actual — the "happening," the materials, including structures and landscapes The painter's use of the photo-image in his conception accurately parallels the photograph's appropriation as a genre of art. All of this is extrinsic to the photograph itself.

With its rise in status, however, the photograph is "read" rather than merely looked at. Images of interest are scrutinized like poems. Predictably, the verbal scrutiny will prove to be what gives the photograph its image. The "readings" will be as subtle, as filled with insight, as bizarre as the talents of the writer. It is hard to imagine a photograph that Susan Sontag could not verbally embellish. Of a W. Eugene Smith photograph, Walker Evans writes: *Welsh Miners* is a memorable and improbable feat: a stroke of romantic realism. Something in the picture doubles back on artifice. The miners are in makeup; their pomade is coal dust. The men are actors, their act is in being themselves. The background stage set is a village you know is there in Wales today."

No question, this commentary adds a new dimension to what we see. Perhaps there is something in all photographs that doubles back on artifice. But Evans would also be the first to say it is better that the photograph have no commentary at all than that it appear to be necessary to the picture. The ambiguity that is natural to the photograph lends itself to conflicting interpretations, but if the viewer's first impression is not his own, he may never come to have one that is. In the photograph this is a real loss for an imaginary gain.

In *First and Last,* a collection of 220 Evans photographs from some 20,000 negatives, words are conspicuously absent. There is no foreword or postword. There are no captions or comments beyond the brief remarks on the jacket. It is a clean, handsome, well-lighted book, appropriate to the photographs. The first was taken in New York in 1928, the last at Brighton Pier, England, in 1973. On turning the pages, however, I found that a few words would have been helpful. These are photographs first,

before they are "images." We are legitimately curious about where the places are and whose face it is. This information is neither irrelevant nor distracting. Whenever we come upon a photograph that is not identified or captioned, the first thing we do is look on the back of it for what is not visible in the picture. In Evans' book we need words to clarify what it is we see and to inhibit much that we might imagine. The two photographs on the jacket are of Evans as a young man, at age twenty-nine, and as an old man, at age seventy-three. I would not have known that without the caption. There is identifying data at the back of the volume printed in type so small it discourages the curious. Words can be as intrusive in their absence as in their presence.

The volume might have been titled *Signs and Portents.* Signs spoke an intimate language to Evans, and I was told by Peter Bunnell that he collected them as objects. The sign and signboard spoke to him as "nature" did not. I first saw an Evans photograph in *Time* magazine: a graveyard of used cars at the side of a road in Pennsylvania. In different accents than it spoke to Evans it also spoke to me. The exact same photograph could be *read* in various ways. What the image maker needs, in all forms of image making, is the confirmation of his own intuitions and Evans provided me, as he did numerous others, with this reassuring shock of recognition. An Evans photograph mattered to all of us.

Some of Evans' photographs are familiar to people who couldn't care less who took them: the portraits in *Let Us Now Praise Famous Men,* the passport-size mosaic of faces crowding the frame of a studio window, a couple on the boardwalk at Coney Island. Evans also worked, for a limited time, for Roy Stryker's Farm Security Administration program, and his "images" will never be free of the aura of the depression. Nor will the photographs themselves ever resolve or clarify their conflicting impressions. A field of junked cars, a man in faded overalls, children in rags, a row of unpainted houses, an unshaved farmhand do not speak to Americans of human realities, but of social conditions to be remedied. When the conditions *are* remedied, they are remarkably less photogenic. There is a conflict of imagery in *Let Us Now Praise Famous Men,* where the words soar into the empyrean but the photographs, happily, remain earthbound. To that extent, the counterpoint is more fruitful than if the words and images were on the same plane.

The great depression was real enough in itself but the hold it still has on our imagination is largely a photographic triumph. These images of hardship, of poverty, of human endurance impose on the recent fiction of history a reality that words can do little to modify or displace. As young photographers have learned, the old and battered, the ugly and depressed are much more photogenic than the new and affluent. Hard times are usually good times for photographers. This aesthetic is rooted in American experience and testifies to our hunger for what is "real", a word that vibrates in our consciousness more persistently than the word "truth". Photography, indeed, is such an American institution that it is difficult to believe we did not invent it. First and last, the photographs of Walker Evans have helped shape our image of what is real, and as this image hardens to a cliché it now obstructs the emergence of what is actually there. Much of what is there is now unseen in photographs that resemble other photographs.

On the jacket of John Szarkowski's *The Photographer's Eye,* a volume of select photographs and well-seasoned comments, there is an anonymous photograph of a bedroom interior at the turn of the century. It is rich with those details we consider revealing, including an optician's chart on the back of the door. The *image* is crisply framed, the point of view as assured as a photograph of Evans, or one of my own. I recognize with a shock that this anonymous photographer was seeing through my eyes and I through his. The similarities of all photographs are greater than their real or imagined differences.

In Walker Evans' book there are no words; in Susan Sontag's *On Photography* there are no photographs. This bizarre polarity comprehends the current photographic scene, where picture taking and making is giving way to analysis and stocktaking. Many young photographers have found themselves more gifted with words than with the camera. In determining what and where photography is at, words are more in ascendant than photographs. The photograph, after all, is just a photograph. Words will determine its meaning and status. Feverishly self-aware, photography now ponders its many selves. As John Szarkowski has commented, the role of the professional has diminished; the personal and the private has expanded. He sees the view as that of the mirror and the window. This is a useful verbal distinction that enshrines the photographer, not the photograph. Mirror, window or wall, the photograph exists; it is a piece of the world's substance and it is more than the source of our self-serving impressions. The true photograph confronts us with all the ambiguities of life itself.

The absence of photographs from Sontag's book is a well-considered decision. Both the writer and the reader are more at home with words. Once an activity of any kind reaches the level of public interest and acceptance, it will undergo this transformation. To *get into words* is the ultimate of critical absorption and appreciation. The breadth and depth of our awareness of photography can be gauged by the absence of photographs in a book or article on the subject. What we want, and what we get, are words. The photographs themselves — like the books, the art, the movies, the events — would complicate and impede the discussion. After all, we still do not know *what* a photograph is.

Just as we cannot accept the photographs of Dachau and Belsen, we cannot *grasp* the image of planet Earth rising on the moon's horizon. There it floats (there we float, that is), chilling and awesome, instinct with the terrors of the first human nightmares. From the first, the gift of sight has been the seedbed of our illusions. The photograph both confirms and mocks us. That's how it is. But *what* it is cannot be photographed.

If Sontag can be faulted in her performance, it lies in the nature of words themselves. How they do go on and on. If the good writer is entitled to be carried away — and Sontag is so entitled — there is still the problem of the benumbled and bedazzled reader. Her facility is intimidating. Numberless photographs, objects and opinions come out of her hopper with a uniform texture. Words accumulate to bury words, as images accumulate to bury pictures. In conversation there are pauses where what is questionable or ponderable can be tempered with a silence or a rebuttal. It is to the reader's disadvantage, curiously, that Miss Sontag lacks or conceals the prejudices of a picture taker. Names, images and associations enrich and confuse our impressions. What is she saying? She is saying what she has said. Like many good books, *On Photography* justifies more rereadings than it will receive. Ignored, if not forgotten, in this performance is the fact that the photograph was once empowered to deal with impressions that words cannot: the ineluctably visible, eye- and mind-boggling world. This image is there before words even as words strain to create a new image. It seems apparent that a frailty in our word-bound culture compels us to reduce *everything* to words. Photography's unique contribution,

the mirrored image of actuality, proves to be, like life itself, merely a point of departure for further speculation. If all we can do is *look* at something, perhaps we would rather not look at it at all. The ultimate inhibition would be to see no more, and no less, than what the camera eye sees.

I find it strange, however, to hear Sontag say, "The main difference between painting and photography in the matter of portraiture still holds. Paintings invariably sum up: photographs usually do not."

Great portraits may well sum up the painter, but they seldom sum up the sitter. What photographs usually do, more than anything else, is authenticate personal appearance and existence. Authentication, not enlargement or interpretation, is what we want. This is sufficient to explain the sudden decline in portrait painting since the first daguerreotype. Manet's portrait of Clemenceau is a painting before it is a portrait, in which "characteristics" have been obliterated. The same is true of Picasso's Stein. The painted portrait neither has nor will displace the photographs by Cameron, Nadar, Hill and Adamson, Southworth and Hawes as well as numberless, often nameless, others. What would we give for a few fair-to-middling album snapshots of Achilles, or Helen of Troy, or Potiphar's wife, or Attila the Hun, or the Wife of Bath, or any human countenance once part of the faceless past? Whose portrait of Lincoln would we prefer to those left us by Brady and Gardner? The sitter might well like to be flattered, but the observer craves reality. In portraiture, once the photograph existed, authenticity takes precedence over talent, and the decline of the painted portrait can be dated from the first one taken by Daguerre. The photo likeness is a piece of nature, like the subject itself.

Puzzlement as to what a photograph actually is still handicaps both photographers and observers. No theory or aesthetic adequately comprehends the ever widening spectrum of photographic practice but the discreet use of the word "image" makes essential distinctions possible. An image is what some photographers are after and we experience their delight when they get it. Rather than another likeness, it has become a thing itself.

It is appropriate that these new images take their place among the objects we value, since they both reveal and enhance our shared awareness of the visible world around us and the invisible world within us. Those photographs that combine the impersonality of the camera eye with the persona of the camera holder will usually commingle the best of these hard-to-reconcile elements. While we continue to grope, like Niepce, for the precise words to capture what a photograph is, we should also acknowledge that the highest praise may be found in the way it eludes us. The ultimate triumph will be to recognize the photograph for what it is.

The most remarkable photographs of our time mirror and probe the macrocosm around us and the microcosm within us, and if a new human is to emerge on this planet some such image will provide one of its icons, a confirmation of the wonder and the shudder of terror that signal an expanding consciousness. We sense in it, and we fear, the necessary destructive element. What it has in mind for us may not be what we have in mind for ourselves.

In the sea of photographs that now surround us and increasingly threaten to engulf us, photography might be likened to the glow of phosphorous where the ship's prow splits the water. Thanks to it, we do see more than the surface. Thanks to it, we do not see more than is there. Not to see more than is there, we learn from photographs, is to see more than enough.

John B. Greene

1832 1856

Beaumont Newhall

Of John B. Greene we know but little, beyond the facts that he died in November 1856 at the age of twenty-four, that he was of American nationality and resident in Paris, that he was a founding member of the Société francaise de Photographie, that he voyaged up the Nile from Alexandria to the Second Cataract in the winter of 1854, that prints from the paper negatives he took on that trip were published later that year in album form, under the title *Le Nil: Monuments, Paysages, Explorations photographiques* by Louis Désiré Blanquart-Evrard at his celebrated *Imprimerie photographique* in Lille and that he also photographed in Algeria.

The calotypes of this "young American" were hailed by the *Photographic and Fine Art Journal* of New York in its October 1854 issue, on the occasion of the acceptance of a collection of them by the Institut de France. His photographs are among the most unusual and beautiful of the quantities of views made in the Middle East since the very birthyear of photography, when the Frenchman Frédéric Goupil-Fesquet and the Canadian Gustave Joly de Lotbiniere brought their daguerreotype apparatus to Egypt to produce the first photographs of the already famous monuments of antiquity. But whereas they and their many followers concentrated on the temples themselves, Greene shows a remarkable sensitivity to the physical environment and the the very lay of the land. He was a master of the distant view. The endless sands, of which so much was written but so little imaged by camera or pencil, dominate his landscapes so that even monuments of incredible scale are dwarfed. The rockhewn colossi of Ramses II at Abu Simbel — the mosques and graves of Moslems — yes, even the noble statue known as Memnon — seem lost in the immensity of the endless desert.

Nor did Greene overlook the features of the Nile herself; the many islands with their date palms, the trees themselves, the rock studded shoals of the cataracts.

His work in Algeria differs as that mountainous land differs from the Nile bed. Greene explores the hill-city of Constantine from many angles, almost as a swooping raven might view it. He fairly throws around its base the sinous Roman aqueduct. He uses his camera with relentless insistence to bring us to the site. He pushes toward us details of masonry, fragmented sculpture and carved epistyle.

Even though his life was inexplicably cut short, John B. Greene is to be numbered among the master photographers of all time.

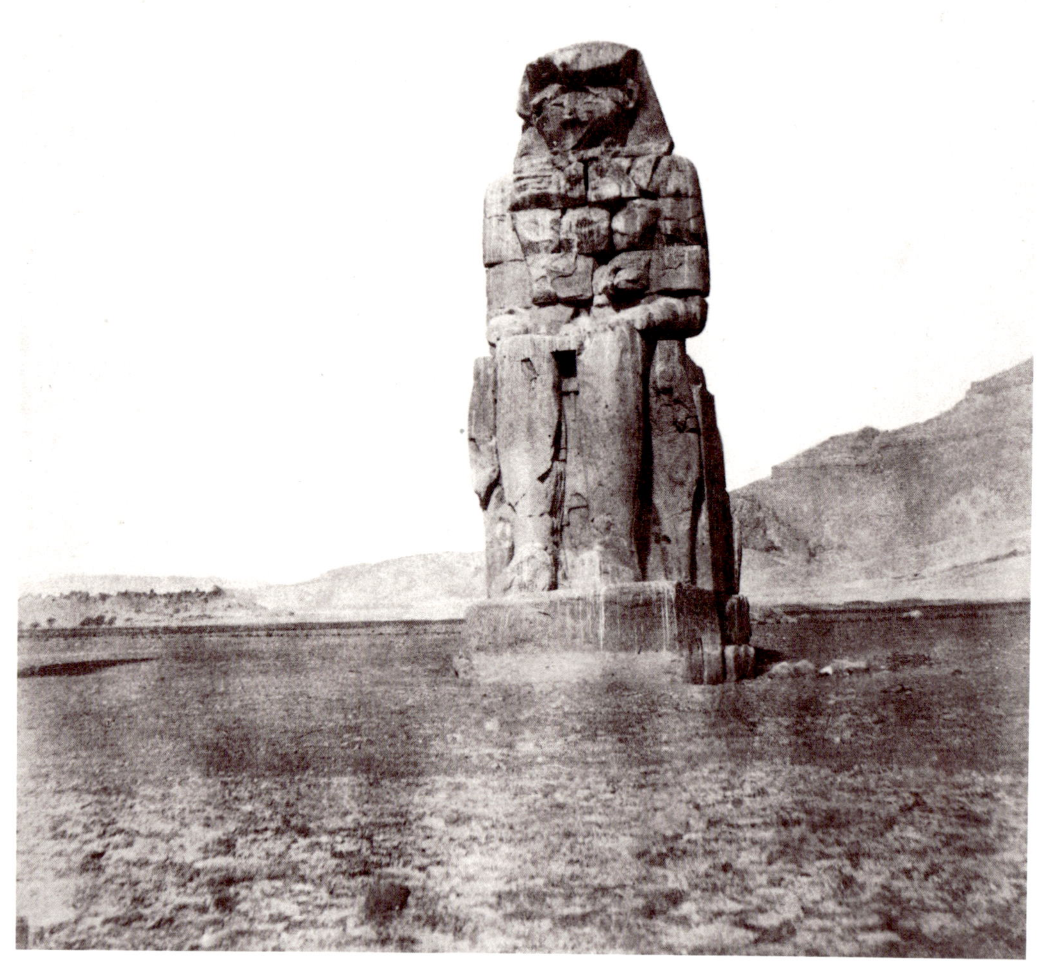

Colossus of Memnon, Egypt, c. 1853-1854

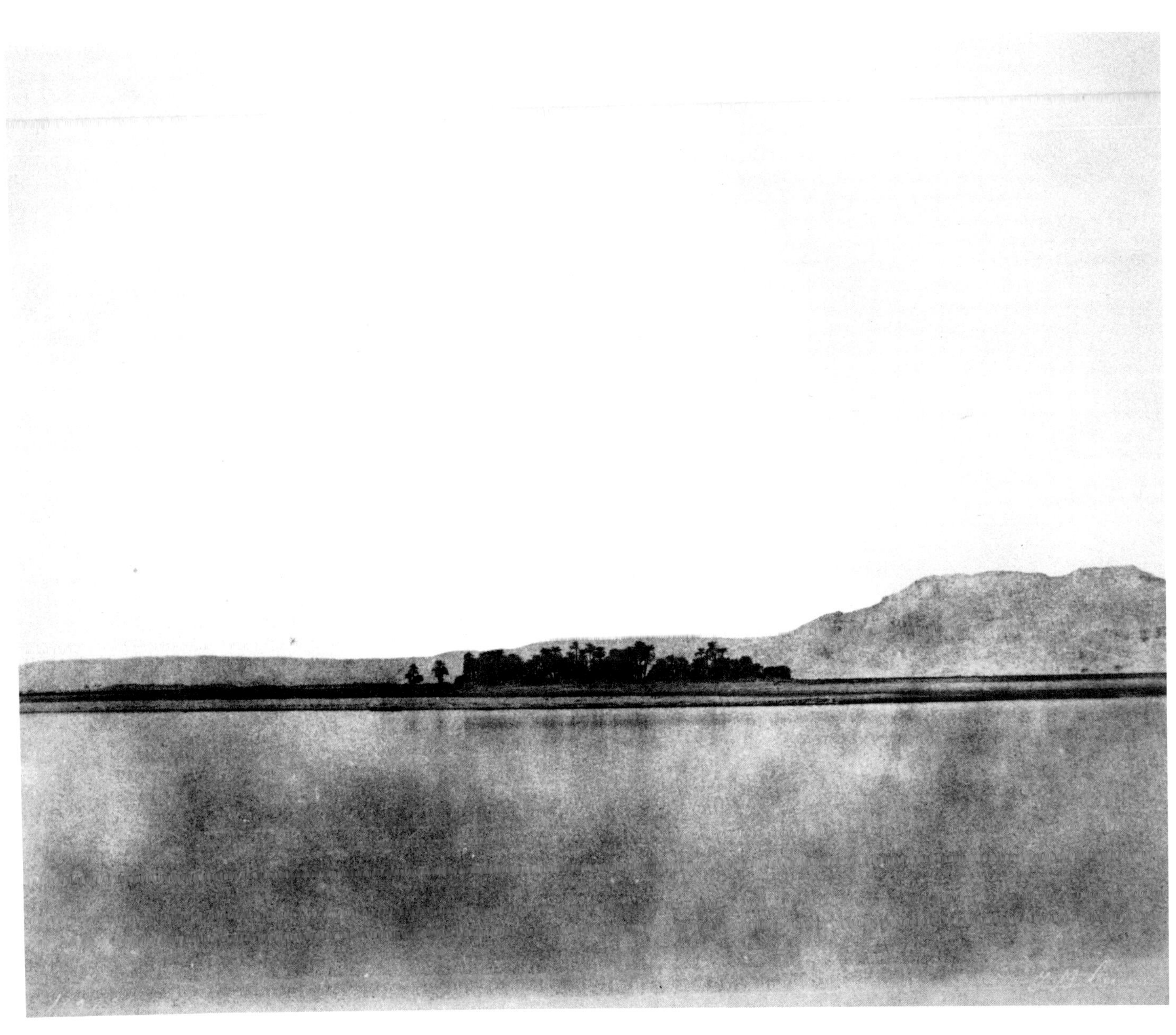

Luxor, Egypt, c. 1853-1854

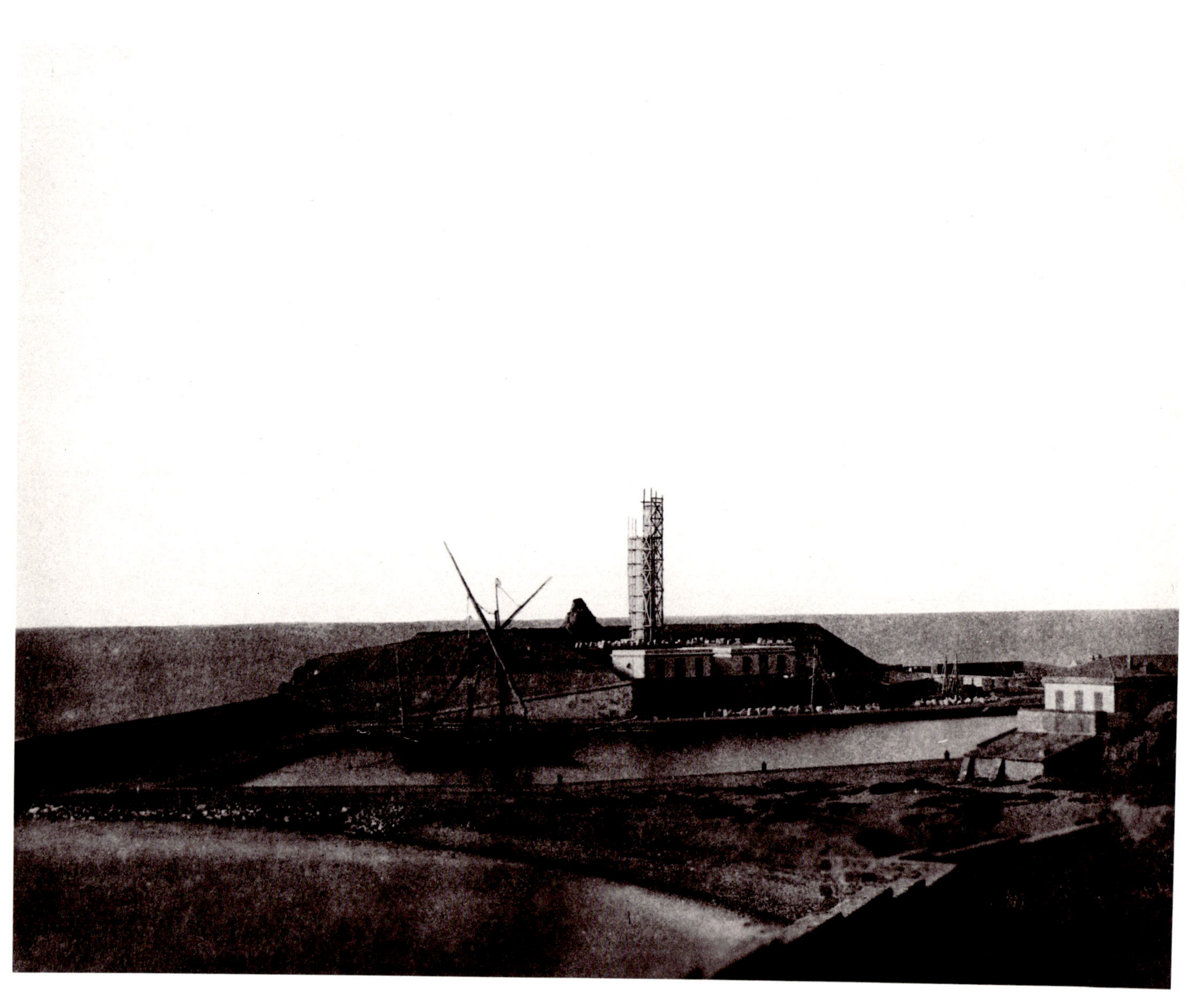

Boat in Harbor, Algeria, c. 1856

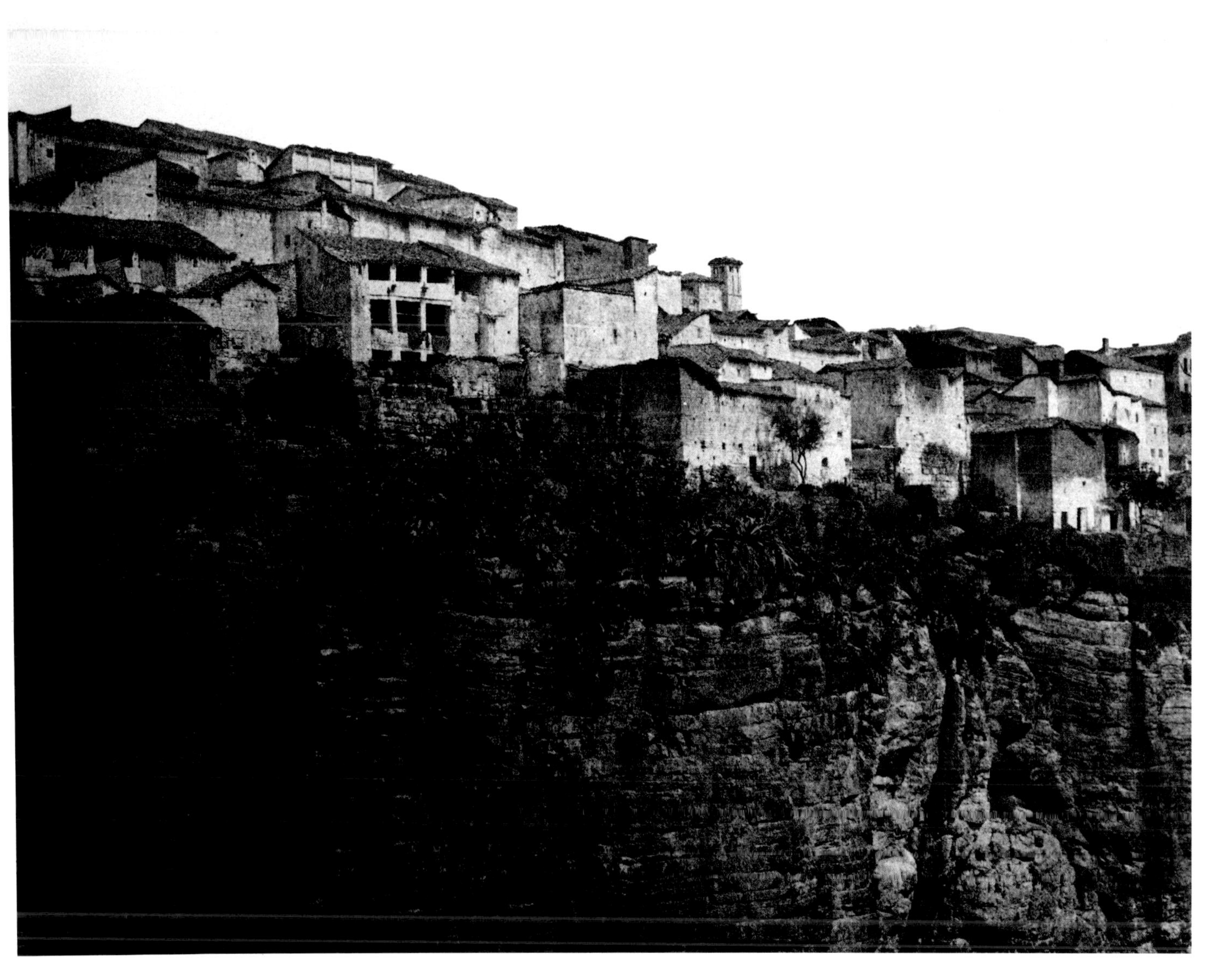

Constantine, Algeria, c. 1856

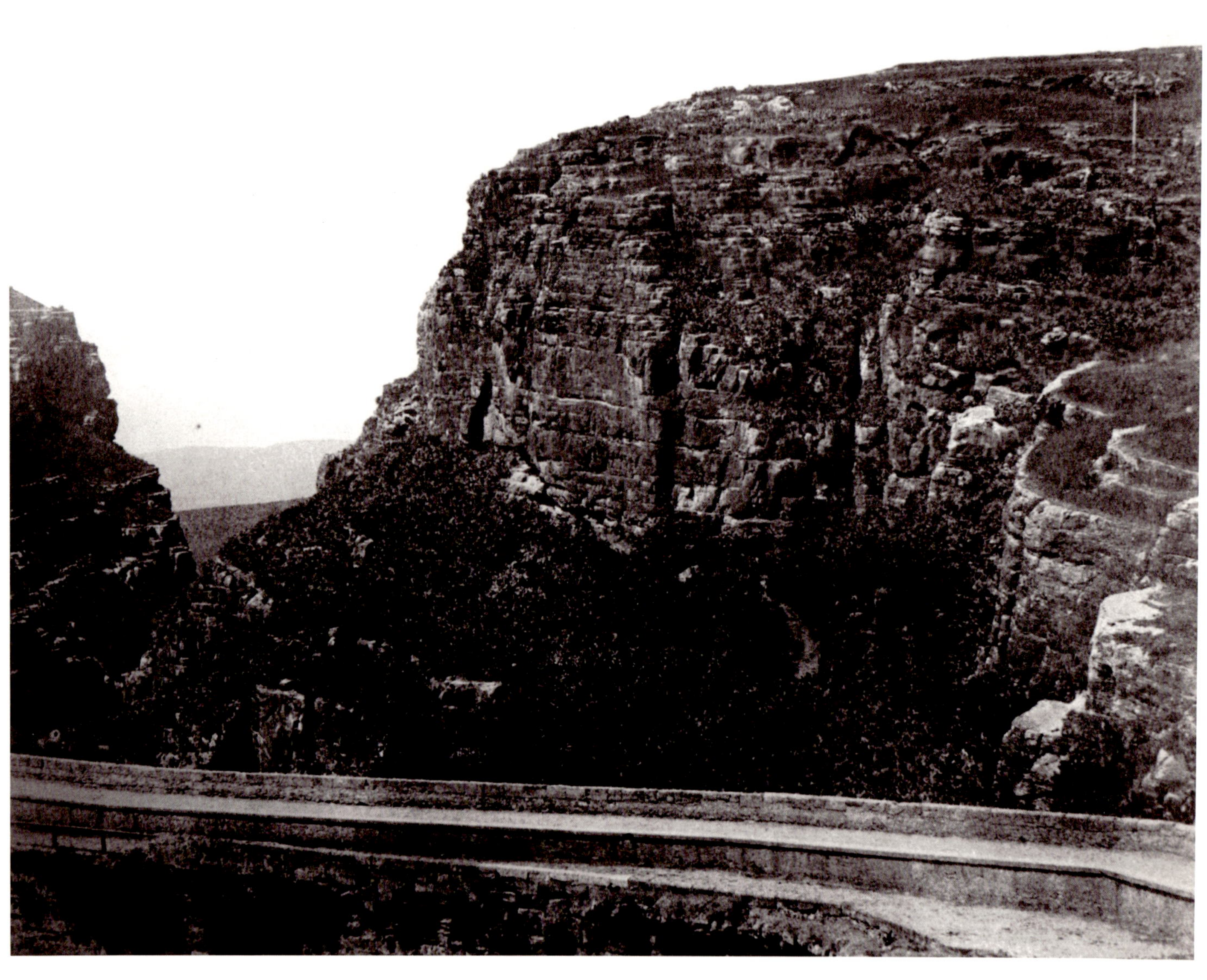

El Kantara Bridge, Constantine, Algeria, 1856

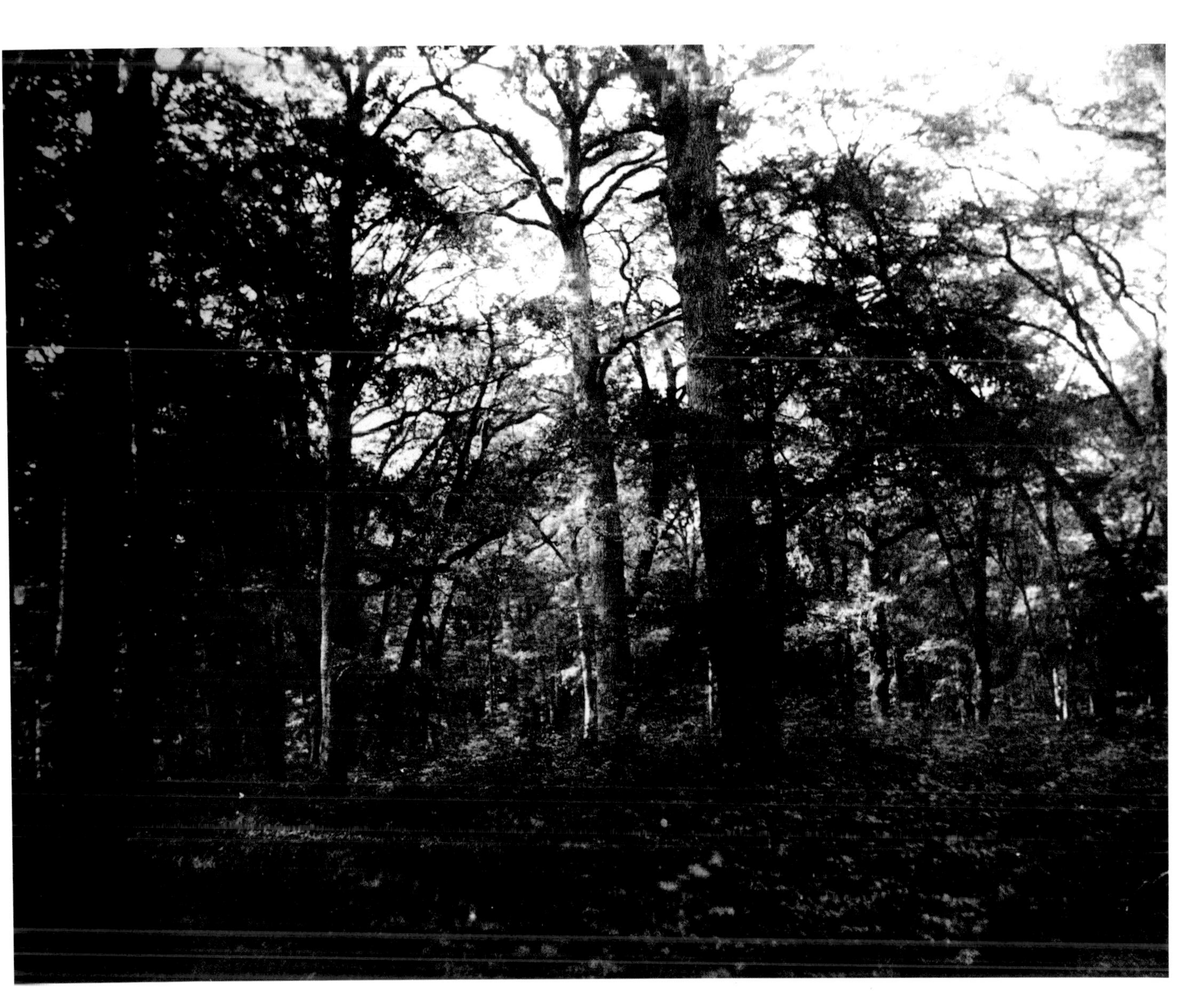

Great Forest of Cedars, West of Teniet-al-Had, Algeria, c. 1856

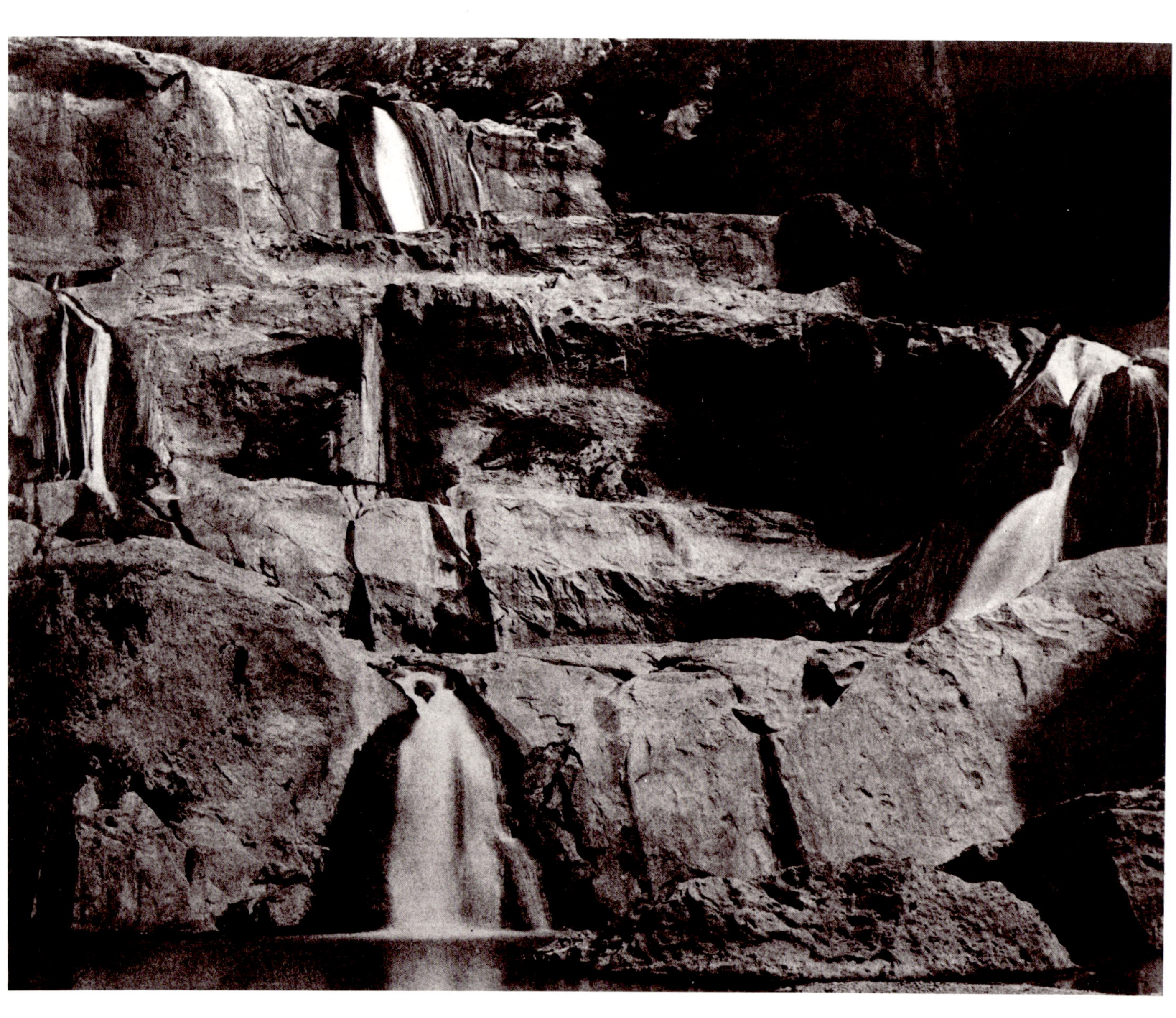

Cascade d'El-Ourit, Tlemcen, Algeria, c. 1856

Imogen Cunningham: Beginnings

Anita Ventura Mozley

In 1903, when Imogen Cunningham, then twenty years old, entered the University of Washington in Seattle, there were no courses offered in either studio art or art history, both interests she had pursued since late childhood. Considering the date, it is not remarkable that no course was offered in photography. She had become acquainted with that medium in 1901, when she was eighteen. She had then sent to the American School of Art and Photography in Scranton, Pennsylvania, for a 4 by 5-inch view camera and instructions on its use.[1] She abandoned interest in it, however, sold the camera and instructions to a friend and devoted herself to other pursuits: her studies and her social life. In 1906 she bought another camera, a 5 by 7-inch view; it was then that she decided to become a photographer. As a result she majored in chemistry at the University and was able, because of her experience with the camera, to help pay her way by making slides for the botany department.

With customary determination she arranged an independent course of study that would prepare her for this career. Her chemistry professor, Dr. Horace Byers, sympathetically helped her plan a curriculum that included reading, practice, chemistry and experiments in photographic technology. She devoted part of her senior year to studying the methods and photographs of Edward S. Curtis, the proprietor of Seattle's most successful portrait studio as well as the memoralist, through his photographs and recordings, of the vanishing customs of North American Indians. After her graduation in 1907, Imogen joined the Curtis Studio, where she made platinum prints from Curtis' negatives and learned the practicalities of the portrait business.

It seems important to emphasize the scientific basis of her training in photography, and to recognize this training as her way of understanding how to use a medium new to her for the artistic expression she had experienced earlier in painting and drawing. Like many of the pictorialist photographers, her visual sense had already been formed in these other media. In school she did not study (could not, in fact) vision or expression; she studied instead the chemistry and optics of photography. She chose an appropriate subject for the paper that completed her course with Dr. Byers: *The Scientific Development of Photography.* In becoming an apprentice in the darkroom of the Curtis Studio she took the next practical step in her career.

While she produced a few portraits of family and friends during this period, most of her energy and interest was devoted to technical mastery, particularly to producing the high-quality platinum prints that were typical of the best in commercial studio production at the time. That platinum was required was itself the result of the pervasive influence of pictorialism. This recent innovation in American commercial studio practice was caricatured by James Montgomery Flagg in the January 1907 issue of *Camera Work,* just when Imogen was beginning to work for Curtis. Flagg's two

drawings contrasted earlier studio practice and Photo-Secession influenced practice. The "Ticklemup Studio" is represented by a hard-edged, shiny-surfaced portrait mounted on a cabinet card inscribed with a typically swash signature. "Blurremout Studio's" production is soft-edged, the narrow tonal scale evidence of Blurremout's use of platinum and the illegible monogram reminiscent of Whistler's source for his butterfly, the Japanese artist's seal.

After two years at the Curtis Studio, Imogen Cunningham sent a portfolio of photographs to the committee that would award the annual scholarship of Pi Beta Phi, the national sorority to which she belonged during her university days. Fifty women competed; Imogen won by unanimous vote. Following this award, on the advice of Dr. Byers, she submitted a proposal to study photochemistry with Professor Dr. Robert Luther of the Technische Hochschule in Dresden, Germany. The Seattle *Post-Intelligencer* quoted Dr. Byers on that occasion: "She is one of the best and most proficient students I have ever had." Her specialty, the article reported, "is children's pictures, and after her course in Dresden, she will take up Photography."

When Imogen went to Dresden in 1909 she considered herself "a beginner and still a school person."[2] She was sure, however, about the kind of photographs she would eventually make. They would be of the sort she had seen reproduced in the April 1907 issue of *The Craftsman.* "I have never forgotten", she later said, "the impact of the photographs I saw in a number of *The Craftsman* . . . It was the work of Gertrude Kasebier that interested me."[3] Particularly, it was *Blessed Art Thou . . . ,* Mrs. Kasebier's famous *tableau-vivant* photograph, the Annunciation theme in modern dress. The text accompanying the reproductions in *The Craftsman,* by the critic Giles Edgerton, was "Photography as an Emotional Art. A Study of the Work of Gertrude Kasebier." Edgerton defined her as an emotional artist because "in every photograph she takes she is expressing her own temperament and life as it has reached her through her imagination and through her growing understanding of humanity." The text must have been as revealing to Imogen Cunningham as the reproductions of Kasebier's photographs. Her own later emphasis on the crucial importance of experience, and of expression over documentation, reflect her early thrill of understanding Kasebier's pictures and Edgerton's text.

She was also an avid reader of *Camera Work,* and on August 10, before leaving Seattle for Dresden, she wrote to the journal asking to be put in touch with Stieglitz, who was in Europe that summer, and with other photographers connected with the Photo-Secession. She did eventually meet Coburn in London and saw Stieglitz and Kasebier in New York on her way home from Europe.

Imogen's year in Germany was, however, devoted to scientific studies and experiments. Although she took her 5

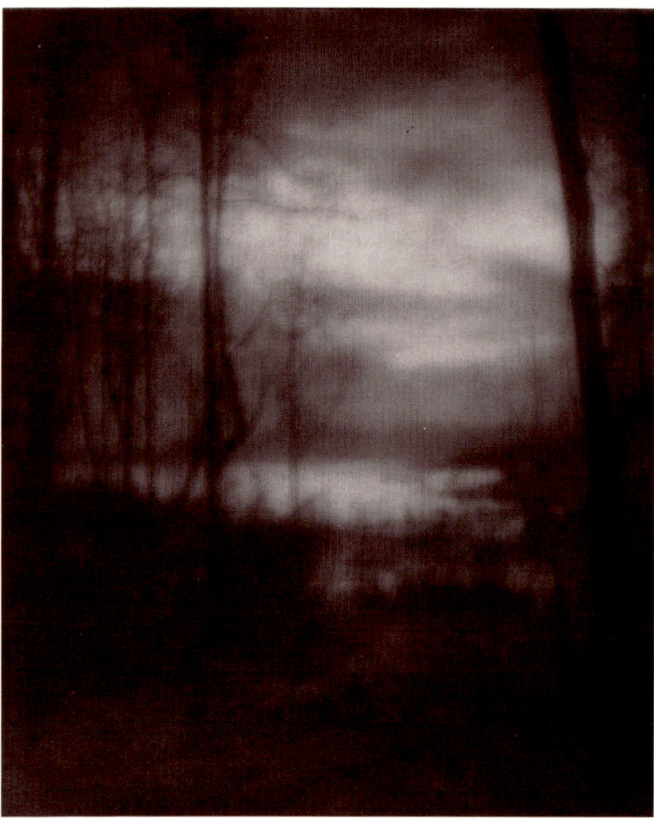

Marsh — Early Morning, 1910, platinum print

by 7-inch view camera and a small Kodak that had been given to her as a going away present by members of the Curtis Studio, she made few photographs in Germany. The only printing she did there, in a four-day session before leaving Dresden in the spring of 1910, was chiefly of negatives she made in Seattle before her trip. Most of her time at the Technische Hochschule (which no longer exists, a victim of the First World War) was occupied with a series of experiments that led to a paper she finished in May of 1910: *About the Direct Development of Platinum Paper for Brown Tones.* After preparing formulae found in the literature for the production of platinum paper, she developed a process of her own that introduced lead salts into a solution containing mercury compounds to produce sepia tones. She concluded that "the addition of lead increases the printing speed and at the same time improves the clarity of the whites." While her method was rigorously scientific, her paper gave hints of her concern with expression. "More certain and beautiful results" were possible when the photographer coated his own paper, and there was an advantage for the photographer in this individual preparation because the formulae "may be altered to accommodate the characteristics of a particular negative."

The time spent in Dresden, the "Florence of Germany", was difficult for her in many ways. She was lonely and short of money; the German ways (or perhaps they were just urban ways) were not her ways. She wrote to her sister Pearl about "a beer-drinking girl with a cigarette in hand — Imagine, the lady is the beloved of one of the associates in the lab and that he is holding the glass." She was twenty-seven and yet unable to look at things at close range in a public lecture because "there were oodles of men . . . I scuttled." Still imbued with family prohibitions, but a bit rebellious, she wrote to Pearl about Christmas festivities which she had earlier described in a letter to her sister Min: " . . . we had three kinds of wine . . . but I drank only champagne. I do hope that [this] letter won't fall into Father's hands — he'd have a fit — if he did —

let him. There are lots of things worse." Her remarks on her personal life and her associations with several lab assistants are tantalizing; perhaps a note to Pearl reveals something of what was going on. "Your Romeo sounded good to me but tell me, is he big and handsome or small and ordinary with brains?" At a ceremony in January only "a very old professor came up to see me."

On a more quotidian level she wrote to her sister Min, "The Germans have only two kinds of dessert, yellow pudding with red sauce & red pudding with yellow sauce, so I have heard, but I have only had the former." But trips to Munich and Berlin, as well as to the opera and to exhibitions of art in Dresden, redeemed the time. She heard Wagner's "Ring" and Puccini's *La Boheme.* She saw Old Master paintings in Dresden's collections and particularly wrote about Raphael's *Sistine Madonna.* She drew from the model at the Dresden Art School and attended lectures on the history of art. She kept a reproduction of *Die Amazone,* a sculpture she had seen on the grounds of the National Gallery in Berlin, at her writing desk because of its "simple and yet so beautiful modernity." Early in her stay she took a skiff down the Elbe to Meissen, where the band played and soldiers sang *Die Wacht am Rhein,* "all the small craft were lighted with Japanese lanterns." During her travels in Germany she visited the important galleries, attended the theater and opera and was a close observer of custom. On her way home she stopped in Paris and in London, where she heard Sylvia Parkhurst and her mother speak in Hyde Park, took a picture of Trafalgar Square and met Coburn.

Perhaps the most important to her of all the exhibitions she saw was the International Photographic Exposition in Dresden, which had opened before she arrived. The critic Charles Caffin called the show "the most complete photographic exhibition ever attempted."[4] The International Group of Art Photographers was among the exhibitors. Chosen by the Austrian photographer Heinrich Kuhn, the group included eleven American, three British, two French and two Austrian photographers, all of them familiar to readers of *Camera Work* and to visitors to Stieglitz' gallery in New York. Steichen exhibited thirty photographs, most of them portraits. Stieglitz was represented by views of New York and by photographs made in France, Holland and the Tyrol. Among the other photographs shown were Annie Brigman's nymphs and naiads, Clarence A. White's interior scenes, Anne Boughton's gentle nudes enacting "The Dawn" or similar themes, and Baron Adolf de Meyer's portraits and close-up still-lifes.

Of them all, Imogen later recalled that De Meyer's photographs made the greatest impression on her.[5] Paul Shumann described them in the October 1909 *Camera Work.* "Each of his portraits has its own individual arrangement, light effects and tonality." Charles Caffin also characterized De Meyer's work as having "naturalness and a gentle harmony"; he was fascinated by the British photographer's "distinguished and remote estheticism." In short, De Meyer's photographs were glamorous, and gave a preview of the glamor that he would contribute, during the 1920s, to the pages of *Vanity Fair.*

While Imogen Cunningham's grasp on social reality eventually overcame her inclination toward dramatic artifice, the beauty of De Meyer's world initially attracted her in Dresden and probably further encouraged the make-believe photographs she produced when she returned to Seattle. On the other hand, she also saw and admired the work of Kathe Kollwitz in Dresden. Kollwitz' powerful social commentary was certainly at the opposite pole from De Meyer's high-style estheticism. It is between these two

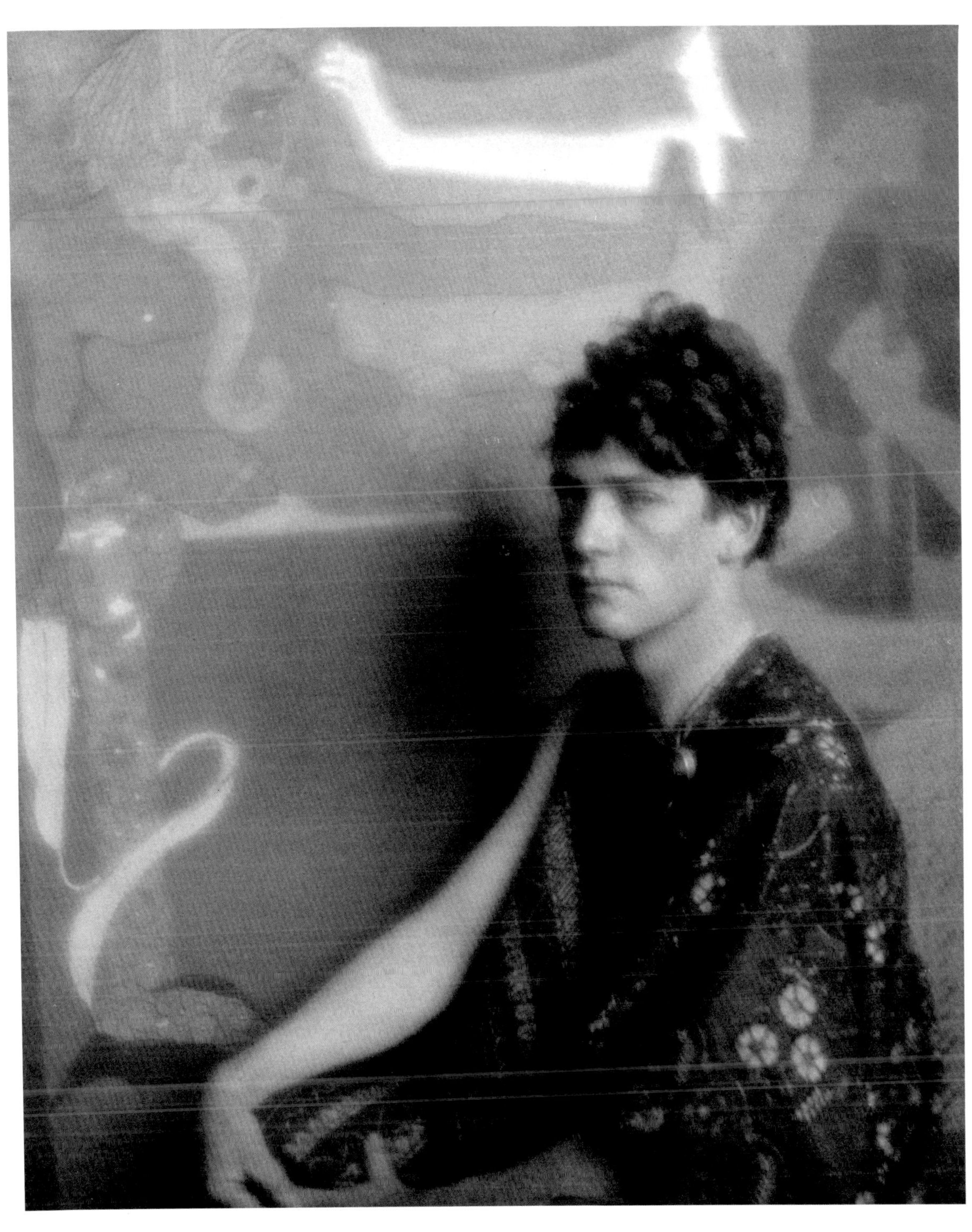

Portrait of John Butler, c. 1912, platinum print

extremes that we can locate Imogen's emerging artistic personality. She later, writing in 1971, recognized these opposing characteristics in herself. "Perhaps my taste lies somewhere between reality and dreamland."

Both of these tendencies were evident in the photographs Imogen made upon her return to Seattle. Studio portraiture occupied her professionally. Her sitters posed in natural light in their own homes, in her comfortable ivy-covered cottage or in the woodsy grounds surrounding it. The three dolls she had bought in Germany as props for photographing children were settled on a pillow near her fireplace; blue fabric was hung about the room, prints and photographs were in frames on the walls. Her customers were disarmed by the attractive simplicity of the place and by her own natural charm and directness. When asked if photography was "a feminine art" she pertly replied, "No, indeed; photography is a matter of individuality, not of sex."[6] She thought that a profession in the arts brought a woman "in contact with the larger interests of the world" and "was bound to have an enlarging effect upon the home." In contrasting the roles available to women, she said:

> I cannot see that a woman of conspicuous leisure grows old more gracefully than does her energetic and creative sister. This is, however, a minor detail in the consideration of a profession, for any work which one loves brings with it a peace and satisfaction for which no amount of repose and elegant leisure can compensate. Being devoted to one's work is much like hearing a great Wagnerian opera with one's soul open. The energy and vitality of life seem for a time sapped, but come back in renewed quantity and quality.[7]

By 1913 Imogen's portrait studio was the choice of Seattle Society, and an exhibition of her photographs that year at the Brooklyn Academy of Arts and Sciences enhanced her fame. In January 1914 she showed one of her first studio portraits (of Mrs. Champney, the handsome aristocrat who, among other titles, wrote *Vassar Girls Abroad*), at "An International Exhibition of Pictorial Photography" held in New York. Among the other exhibitors were James Craig Annan, Alvin Langdon Coburn, Robert Demachy, De Meyer, Frederick H. Evans, Arnold Genthe, Kasebier, George Seeley, Clarence White and Paul Strand. To a person who had considered herself a beginner four years earlier this must not have seemed bad. She was also honored in her home town; the Post-Intelligencer called her "the young Seattle woman who is amazing art critics of the U.S. with her continual successes with the camera."[8] Evidently spurred on by her recognition she wrote early in that year to Alfred Stieglitz, telling him about her forthcoming exhibition in Brooklyn and avowing her ambition to have her photographs published in *Camera Work*. It was an ambition that went unsatisfied; in later life she characterized the Stieglitz group as "elitist".

Outside of the portrait studio she "fooled around" for herself, exploring the glamor of make-believe she had sensed in seeing De Meyer's work in Dresden and printing the resulting view camera negatives in platinum. She posed her friends, the painters John Butler and Clare Shephard, in diaphanous veils and wrapped them in kimonos or in lengths of fabric patterned after William Morris' designs. She hired a family — parents and young daughter — to pose naked for her. They went to the misty woods where she stood them by reflecting pools in poses arranged to illustrate Morris' 1894 prose romance *The Wood Beyond the World*, Swinburne's poetry or Elizabeth Barret Browning's *Sonnets from the*

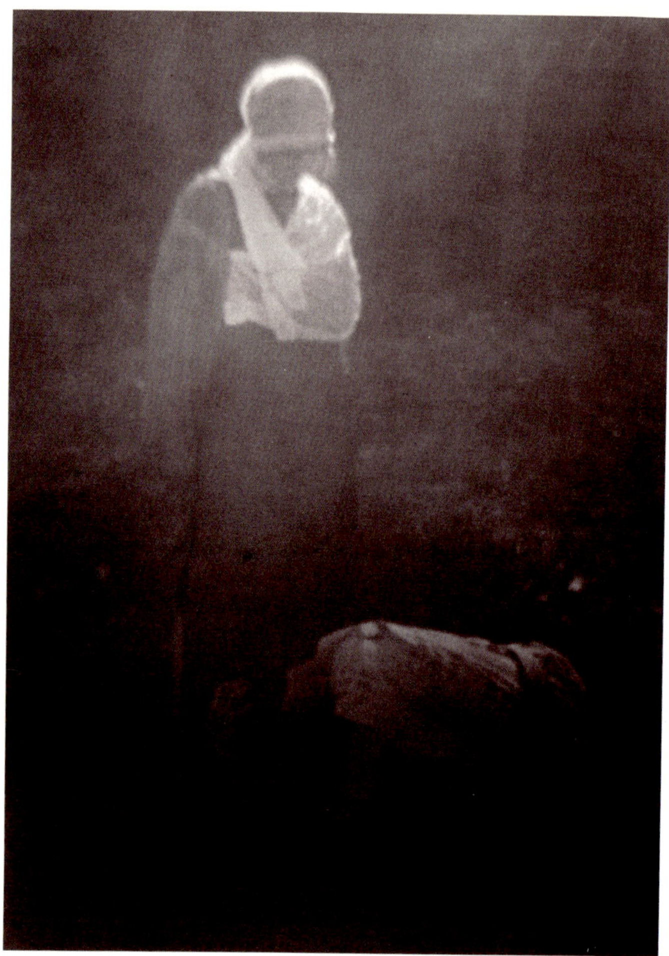

Conscience, c. 1910-1912, platinum print

Portuguese. She also dealt with moral themes in photographs she called *Conscience* and *Eve Repentant.* In a note written in 1910 she instructed herself to "do one to *The Clouded Mirror*/mirrored shape of a nude."

The illustrations to Morris are appropriate in spirit, not literal. Imogen loved his *Wood Beyond the World,* a romance that takes place in a distant land richly covered with flowers and woods, where nude figures and enchantresses enact allegories of good and evil. It was in this combination of fantasy and morality that she found a subject congruent with her own romantic idealism.

After her marriage to the artist Roy Partridge in February 1915 Imogen had a willing model for nude studies. He sat naked on a sheet of ice by a pool on Mt. Rainer; she called it *The Faun,* a tribute, probably, to Nijinsky's sensational 1912 performance in Stravinsky's *L'Apres-Midi.* Or he posed grasping at twisted bare branches, or running through spiky woods, his body outlined in bright sunlight. It seems a far cry from the children's pictures that had been predicted earlier in the Seattle *Post-Intelligencer.*

These photographs were shown in Seattle in November 1915 under the auspices of the Seattle Fine Arts Society, of which both Roy and Imogen Partridge were members. A long, narrow invitation on grey art paper, folded once, announced the exhibition in a typeface reminiscent of those used by William Morris. The chaste-looking catalogue gave the titles of Imogen's photographs, including *Pan in the Mountains,* as well as those of the etchings, miniatures and paintings by the three other artists, Roy Partridge, Claire Shephard and John Butler. Among her photographs was one of the family she had hired in 1910; the father's genitals are clearly revealed and the figures are reflected in the pool in which they stand. This photograph was among those reproduced full-page in the Seattle *Town Crier*, a journal that had followed Imogen's career with approving comment. Seattle, however, was outraged and made its outrage so effectively heard that she packed away the offending photographs and negatives for fifty-five years.

The 1915 exhibition, in effect, was a summation of Imogen Cunningham's early work. The last show of a pre-war romance, it marked the end of a period. By 1917 the idyll was ended. Although Morris' *Wood Beyond the World* was, ironically, one of the most popular books in the trenches of Europe, Imogen moved on, to another place to do other work. It was not until 1970, toward the end of her life, that the beginning phase of her career in photography became widely known. In that year she received a Guggenheim Fellowship to print old negatives, among them those she had made with her friends in Seattle's misty woods. What did she think of her beginnings? In 1964 she wrote of her early photographs, "They are from what I call my 'dream period', when I read William Morris and thought I understood poetry, especially Swinburne." She described her Guggenheim work as "printing my past."

NOTES

1. One print that derives from this first period of her photography still exists: *Marsh — Early Morning*, now in the Alvin Langdon Coburn Collection of the International Museum of Photography at George Eastman House, Rochester. She made the print and sent it to Coburn after her meeting with him in London in 1910. He found it "charming . . . the sky is so luminous." Years later she wrote to Minor White that, lacking a negative, she had made an enlarged negative from a sharp 4 by 5-inch photo and made it soft (damn it) and made a platinum print." It would be interesting to find the original sharp print of *Marsh*, 1901, from which she made the soft print in 1910.

   This essay is an excerpted and revised version of one prepared for publication in 1978. The quotations and information are, unless otherwise noted, from the Imogen Cunningham papers and correspondence held by The Archives of American Art, and are published with the permission of her estate.

2. "Imogen Cunningham, Portraits, Ideas and Design", an interview conducted by Edna Tartaul Daniel, University of California General Library, Berkeley, Regional Cultural History Project, 1961, p. 51. Quotations from this interview are used with the permission of the Director, Bancroft Library, University of California, Berkeley.

3. E.T. Daniel interview, p. 18. *The Craftsman*, published by a guild of American cabinetmakers, metal and leather workers, dedicated its first issue, October 1901, to the life, art and influence of William Morris, the British designer, typographer and political philosopher. The guild was formed and the journal published to "provide and extend the principles established by Morris, in both the artistic and the socialist sense." Simplicity, individuality and "dignity of effect" were the goals of the guild. *The Craftsman* first published photographs in its January 1906 issue, in which the "New Art Photography" of Clarence A. White was discussed. Other Secessionist photographers were presented in following issues. While one need not become frenzied about dates, it is important to try to pinpoint them in any discussion of an artist's beginnings. Imogen herself made a comment on the beginnings of her career in a letter of 1956 about an article published on her work in the May 1951 *Modern Photography*. "There are of course some slight discrepancies, such as 'began my career in 1901 when I got my first camera from the International Correspondence School at Scranton, Pennsylvania.' That is a good many years from the truth. I did get a camera and I did work at it, but I had a great many years of school in between that time and when I first set up shop for myself. That was in 1910."

4. C.H. Caffin, "Some Impressions from the International Photographic Exposition, Dresden", *Camera Work 28*, October 1909.

5. E.T. Daniel interview, p. 51.

6. E. I. Halderman, "Successful Seattle Business Women", Seattle *Post Intelligencer*, n.d. (1913).

7. F. H. Maschmedt, "Imogen Cunningham, An Appreciation", *Wilson's Photographic Magazine*, March, 1914, pp. 97-99.

8. I. H. Rafter, "A Brief Account of the Work of Imogen Cunningham of Seattle", Seattle *Post Intelligencer*, May 11, n.d. (c. 1914).

1980 Exhibitions

The following exhibitions were presented in The Friends of Photography's Wynn Bullock Gallery in Carmel, California, during 1980. Depending on the size of the individual prints, each exhibition contained sixty to eighty photographs.

January 11 to February 10
PHOTOGRAPHS BY ROY DeCARAVA

February 15 to March 16
CARLETON E. WATKINS
PHOTOGRAPHS OF THE COLUMBIA RIVER
AND OREGON

March 21 to April 20
THE DIANA SHOW, PICTURES THROUGH
A PLASTIC LENS
Jim Alinder, Susan Backman, John Carnell, Larry S. Ferguson, Valorie Fisher, Brian Forrest, Sally Gall, Carson Graves, Gene Groppetti, Stephen M. Guenther, David Hamilton, John D. Hansen, Sindy Kipis, Gary Kolb, T. M. Langdon, Lili Lauritano, Dennis Letbetter, Eric Lindbloom, Carl Martin, Charles Marut, Keith Mayton, Dan McCormack, Jack Murphy, Ardine Nelson, David Nester, Jeffrey A. Newman, Dirk E. Park, Thomas J. Petit, Duane Powell, Peter Reiss, Nancy Rexroth, Rich Rollins, Victoria Lyon Ruzdic, James Sandall, Lauren Shaw, Cindy Sirko, Peter Stazione, Brian D. Taylor, Joanne Tracy, Robyn Wessner, Sharon Wickham, Graydon Wood, Ann Zelle.

Organized as a traveling exhibition, *The Diana Show* will be shown at twelve galleries throughout the country before the end of 1981.

April 25 to May 25
THREE APPROACHES TO VISUAL BIOGRAPHY
Photographs by William DeLappa and Marcia Resnick
Photoetchings by John Takami Morita

May 30 to July 6
AERIAL PHOTOGRAPHS BY WILLIAM GARNETT

July 11 to August 10
PHOTOGRAPHS BY DIANE KEATON AND
TRICIA SAMPLE

August 15 to September 14
1980 MEMBERS EXHIBITION
David Aschkenas, Dorothy Barnett, Ruth-Marion Baruch, Robert D. Beard, Arthur L. Berger, Charles E. Bogard, Joseph Boudreau, Harrison Branch, Lawrie Brown, Robin Brown, Jerry Burchfield, Marsha Burns, Michael Burns, Kenneth Cain, Jo Ann Callis, David Covey, Aldo Davanzo, Robert Dawson, Joel Degrand, Rita Dibert, Allen E. Dutton, Greg Erf, Larry S. Ferugson, Kurt Fishback, Klaus Frahm, Luciano Franci de Alfano, Ellen Gibson, Vincent Giordano, Lyle Gomes, Vahe Guzelimian, Bob Haft, Douglas Hill, Harry J. Ibach, Andrea Jennison, Pirkle Jones, Tim Kilby, Gary Kolb, Mark Krastoff, Sara Leith, Nathan Lerner, Stu Levy, Cynthia Lewis, Mati Maldre, Grayson Mathews, Elliott McDowell, Lawrence McFarland, Joan C. Netherwood, Ted Orland, Olivia Parker, Jeannie Pearce, Martha Pearson, Michael Peven, J. P. Pietrzak, Emmy Reese, John Scarlata, Fred Scheel, Mark Schwartz, John Sexton, Lee Silverman, Robert Stiegler, Frances Storey, Lou Stoumen, Karen M. Strom, Allen Swerdlowe, Jerry Takigawa, Brian D. Taylor, Alan Teller, Charles Traub, Todd Walker, Patricia White, Marion Post Wolcott, Don Worth.

September 19 to October 19
IMAGES FROM WITHIN, THE PHOTOGRAPHS
OF EDMUND TESKE

October 24 to November 30
NEW LANDSCAPES, PART I
David Avison, Morley Baer, Winston Swift Boyer, Robert K. Byers, Walter Chappell, Mark Citret, Peter de Lory, King Dexter, Jay Dusard, Larry S. Ferguson, Neil Folberg, William Garnett, Richard Garrod, William Giles, Henry Gilpin, Lyle Gomes, Art Grice, Andrea Jennison, Michael Johnson, Pirkle Jones, Robert Glenn Ketchum, Stuart D. Klipper, Lynn Lown, Lawrence McFarland, Jim Needham, Edward Ranney, Charles Roitz, Alan Ross, John Sexton, Clinton Smith, Michael A. Smith, Mary Swisher, Mathias Van Hesemans, Laura Volkerding, Huntington Witherill, Don Worth.

December 5 to January 11, 1981
NEW LANDSCAPES, PART II
Robert Adams, Laurie Brown, Stephen Berens, Linda Connor, Joe Deal, Robbert Flick, Deborah Flynn, Lee Friedlander, Frank Gohlke, Wanda Hammerbeck, Eric Johnson, Harold Jones, Mark Klett, Jean Locey, Martha Madigan, Susan Makov, Joe Maloney, Richard Margolis, Barbara Mensch, Tom Millea, Richard Misrach, Barbara Noah, Ted Orland, Bruce Patterson, John Pfahl, Tricia Sample, Gail Skoff, Jerry N. Uelsmann, Gwen Widmer.

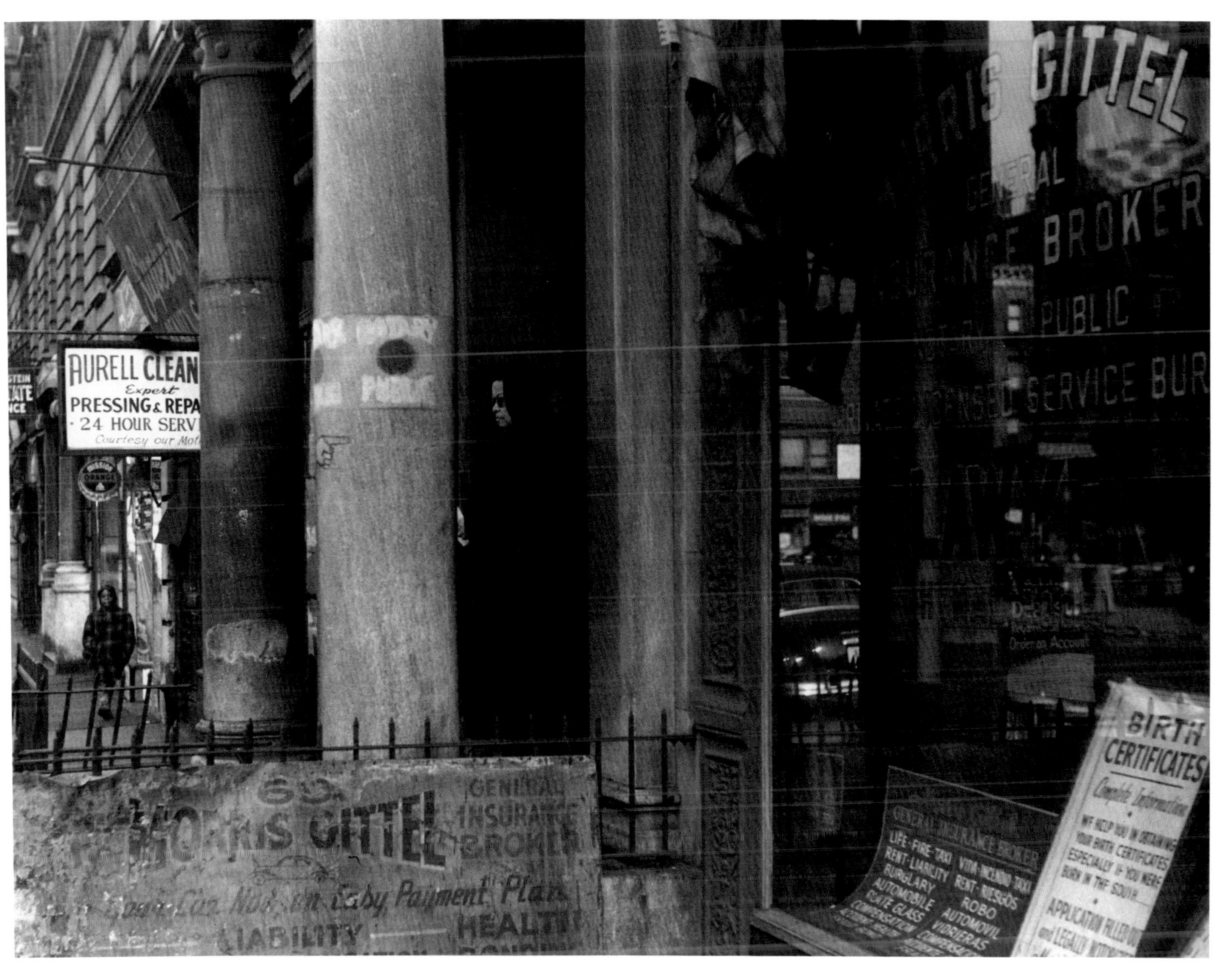

Roy DeCarava
Gittel, New York, 1950

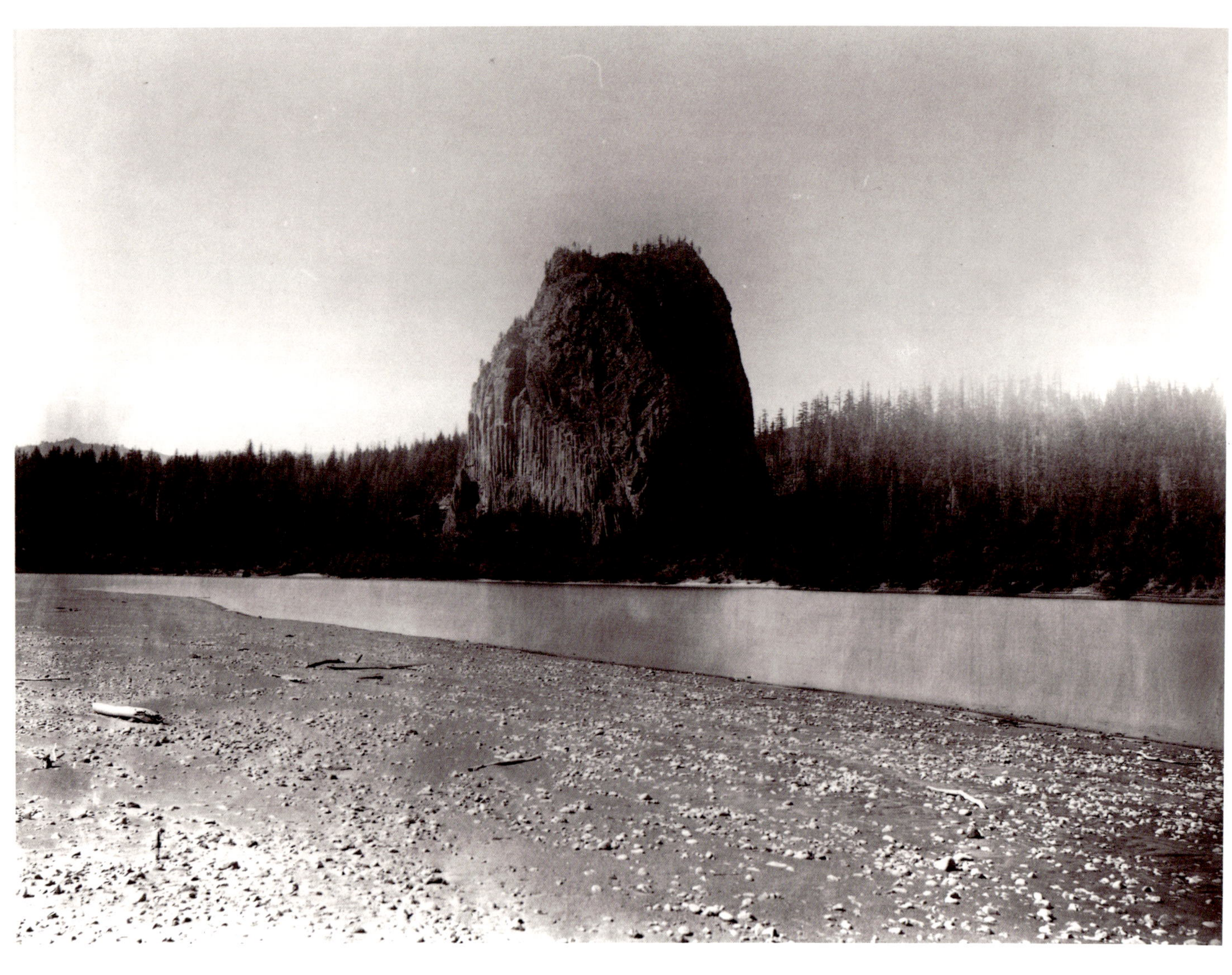

Carleton E. Watkins
Castle Rock, Columbia River, 1867

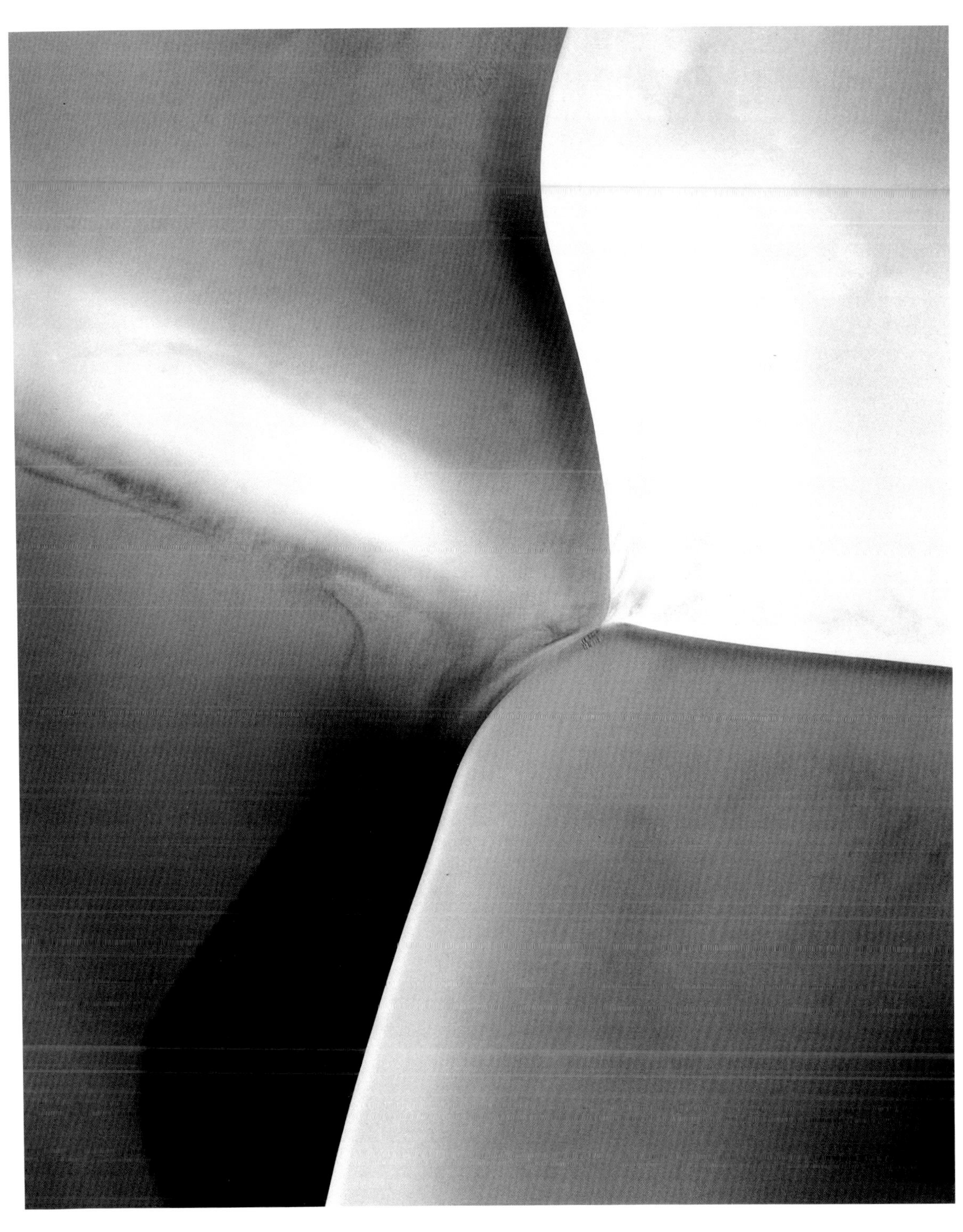

William Garnett
Four Sided Dune, Death Valley #2, 1954

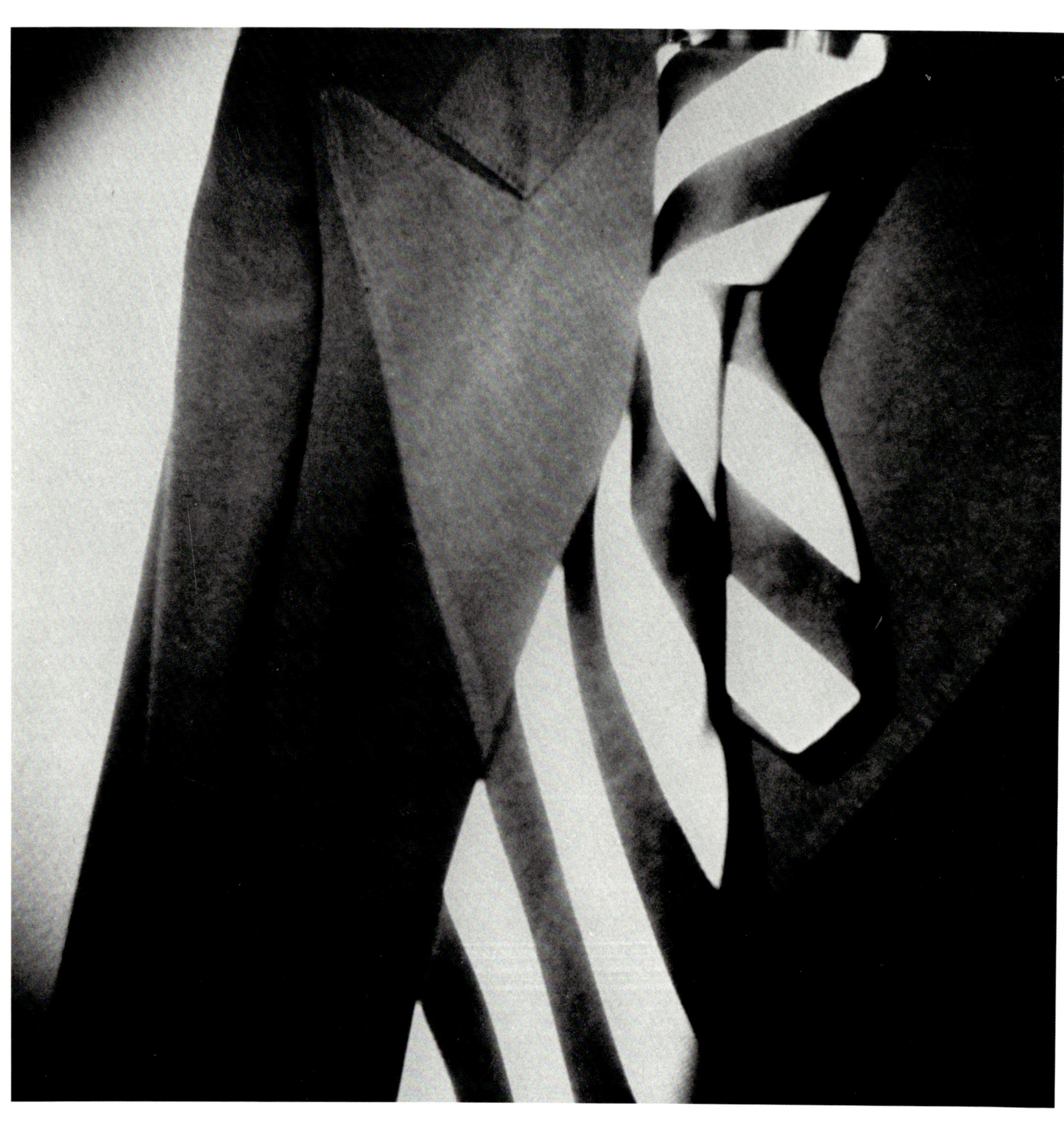

Dirk E. Park
Untitled, from The Diana Show

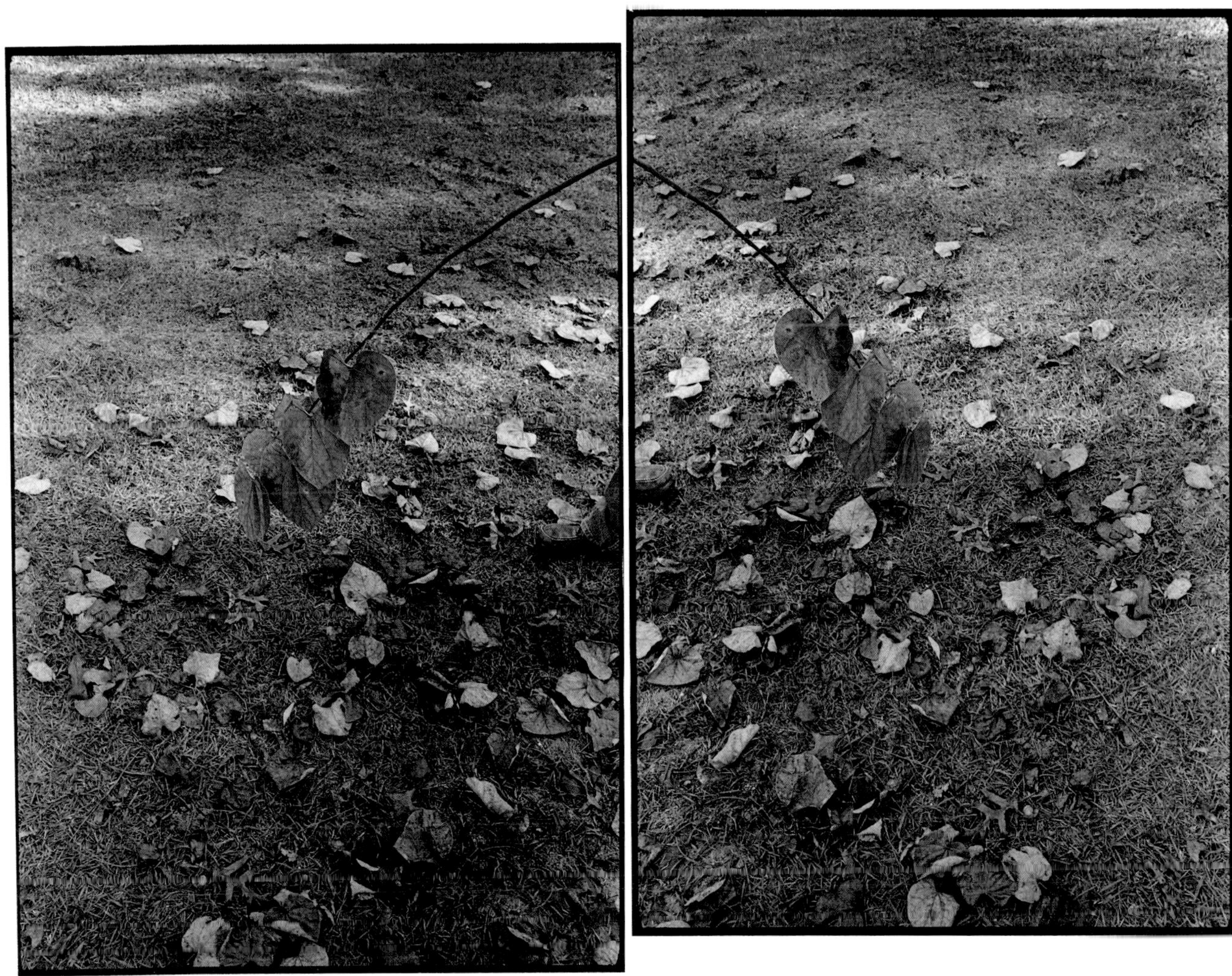

Tricia Sample
Untitled, 1980

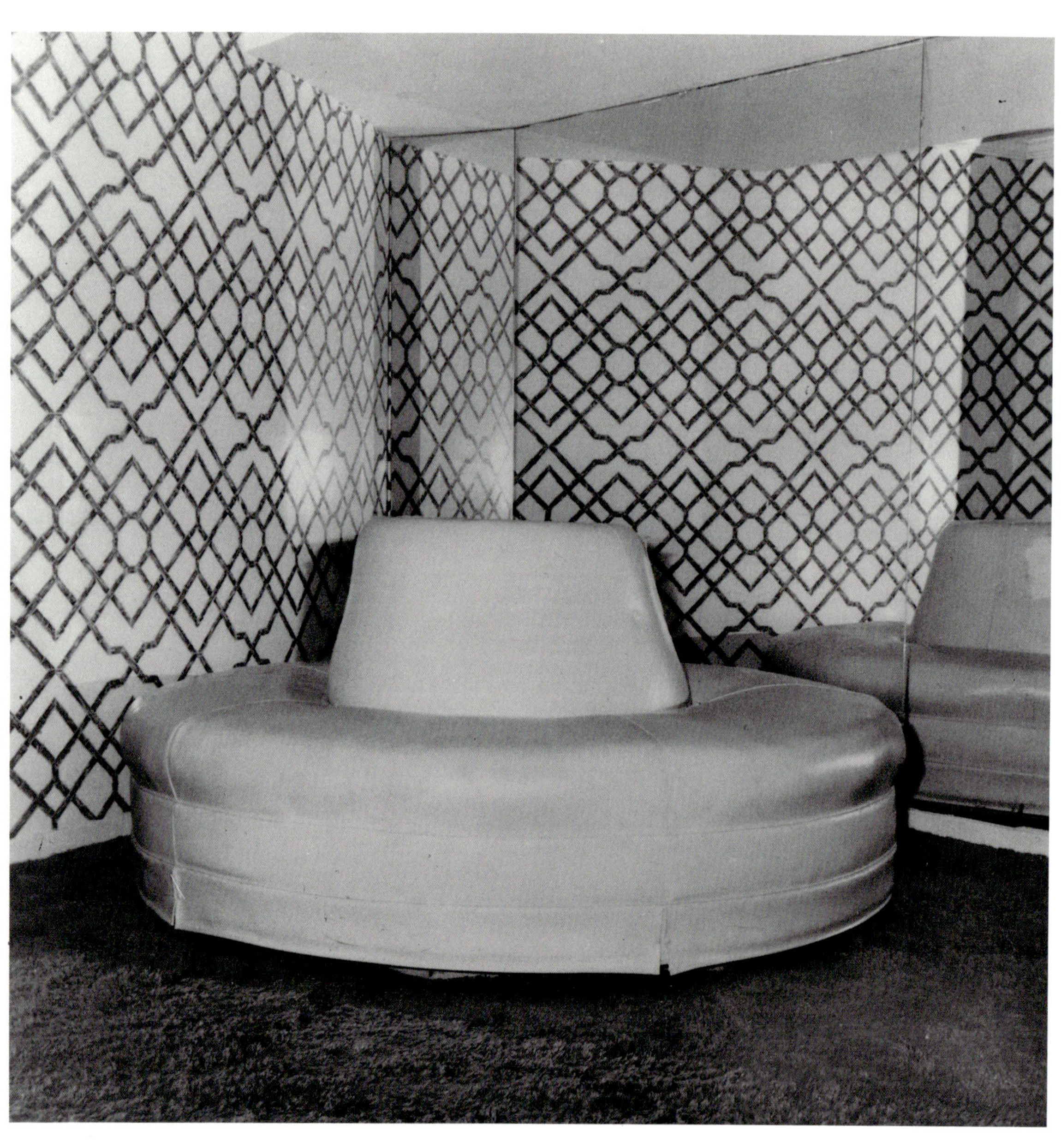

Diane Keaton
The Fountainbleau Hotel, Miami Beach

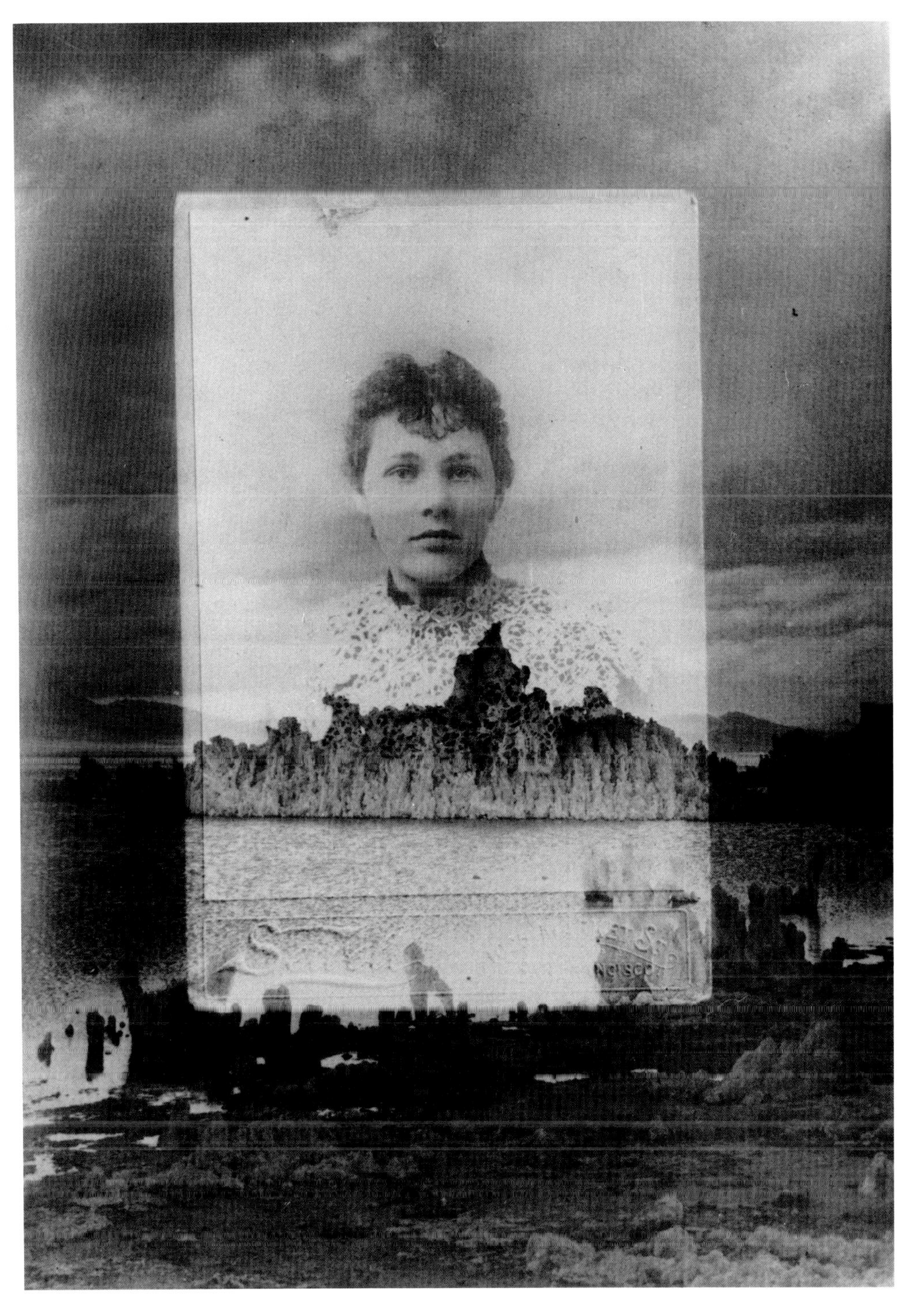

Edmund Teske
Frances Montrose, Great Grandmother, Composite, 1976
From the sequence Mono Lake

Contributors

HARRY CALLAHAN began his involvement with photography in 1938 and has served as head of the photography programs at both the Institute of Design in Chicago and the Rhode Island School of Design. His color and black-and-white photographs have been presented in more than 30 one-artist exhibitions. During 1980 two major books were published documenting his work: *Water's Edge* (Callaway Editions) and *Harry Callahan: Color* (Matrix).

LEE FRIEDLANDER studied with Edward Kaminsky at the Art Center in Los Angeles from 1953 to 1955. Since that time he has become one of the most prolific and influential contemporary photographers. He received fellowships from the John Simon Guggenheim Memorial Foundation in 1960, 1962 and 1977 and a Photographer's Fellowship from the National Endowment for the Arts in 1972. A book of his flower and tree photographs will be published during 1981.

MARK KLETT is presently Assistant Director of Photography at the Sun Valley Center for the Arts and Humanities. He received is MFA degree in 1977 from the Visual Studies Workshop in Rochester, New York. From 1977 to 1979 he served as Chief Photographer for the *Rephotographic Survey Project,* a comparative photographic survey of the American West.

WRIGHT MORRIS is a native of Nebraska who has drawn fully on his experience of Mid-America in his photographs and novels. Over the past four decades he has produced more than two dozen volumes of fiction, criticism and photographs. He has received three Guggenheim Fellowships and was the 1956 winner of a National Book Award. *Photographs, Images and Words* was first published in a slightly different form in *The American Scholar,* Autumn, 1979.

ANITA VENTURA MOZLEY is currently Curator of Photography at the Stanford University Museum of Art. A former contributing editor for *Arts Magazine,* her critical articles have appeared in many publications. She provided a major introduction for the three-volume edition of Edweard Muybridge's *Animal Locomotion* (Dover, 1979).

BEAUMONT NEWHALL teaches the History of Photography at the University of New Mexico. A former Director of both the George Eastman House and the Photography Department of the Museum of Modern Art, he is the author of over 500 articles and books on photography. He is the editor of *Photography: Essays & Images* (Museum of Modern Art, 1980), a collection of articles drawn from historical sources in photography. He is presently revising his standard work, *The History of Photography.*

The Friends of Photography

The Friends of Photography, founded in 1967, is a not-for-profit membership organization with headquarters in Carmel, California. The Friends actively supports and encourages creative photography through wide-ranging programs in publications, grants and awards to photographers, exhibitions, workshops, lectures and critical inquiry. The publications of The Friends, a major benefit received by members of the organization, emphasize contemporary photography yet are also concerned with the criticism and history of the medium. They include a monthly newsletter, a quarterly journal and important large-format photography books. Membership is open to everyone. To receive an informational membership brochure write to the Membership Director, The Friends of Photography, Post Office Box 500, Carmel, California 93921.

SUSTAINING MEMBERS

Martin Ackerman, Ansel Adams, Gary Adams, Chris Adamson, Adeba Photography, Dwight Agan, Jesse Alexander, James Allison, Amon Carter Museum of Western Art, Adolph Amster, Paul Bandt, Bruce Barnbaum, E. A. Basse, Ira Bates, Louis Bencze, Robin Benezra, Lynette Berg, Ralph Berlovitz, Neil Berzak, J. E. Bethune, Jean-David Beyer, Gay Block, Debra Bloomfield, Charles Bogard, Barbara Bordnick, Phillips Bourns, Mike Bowman, Steve Bradley, Art Brewer, Lawrance Brown, Steve Bruno, Howard Bucquet, Dr. and Mrs. Robert Bunnen, Robert Byers, George Byrne, Thomas Carcaterra, Carmel Answering Service, Chip Carroll, Nicki Casado, Harry Casimir de Rham, David Catsman, Central Computer Exchange, Guy

Chambers, Thomas Chin, Ann Marie Chinnery, Lauren
Clark, James Cloutier, Gordon Cohen, Richard Collins,
William Collins, Dr. and Mrs. L. Comfort, Robert Connan,
Mariana Cook, David Cooper, Alfred Corbett, Beth Cotner,
Warren Coville, H. M. Cresap, Barbara Crooker, Nicholas
Culkowski, P. O. Dahlman, George Dalsheimer, Wallace
Danielson, Louis DeCarlo, Albert DeVito, Frank Delph,
Ray Dennis, King Dexter, Peter DiPietro, J. M. Douglas,
Karl Drayton, Christopher Dungan, Arnold Dunkelman,
John Dunker, Earl Dyess, Charles Easley, Regan Ehrman,
Terry Engelstad, Jilian Eubank, Bernard Faber, John
Faerber, Dr. Ronald Ferris, Mrs. E. C. Finch, Duross
Fitzpatrick, Joseph Folberg, Robert and Nancy Fortner,
Dr. B. B. Frankel, J. R. Funk, Kent Furlow, Michael
Furman, Leif Garbisch, James Garland, Betsy Gates, Mike
and Colleen Gaylord, Ellen Ross Gibson, Robert Giguere,
Arnold Gilbert, Jeffrey Glasser, Jack Glenn, Orville Golub,
Ricardo Gonzalez, Seymour Goodstein, Hal Gould, Roger
Graetz, Jo Ann Green, Ursula Gropper, Mrs. Walter Haas,
Ron Hagerthy, William Hamm, Mrs. Arthur Hanisch, B. V.
Harris, Jerry K. Hart, Charles Henningsen, Richard Henry,
Mark Hirschman, Nancy Holdsworth, Andy Hollar,
Harrison Horblit, Julianne Howe, Charles Hrbek, C. A.
Hudson III, James Hudson, Herbert Inglove, Arthur
Jacobson, Jim Jacquin, Warren Jaeger, Albert Jenny, W.
Kent Johns, Diana Johnson, Reverdy Johnson, Terry
Jonasson, Allen Jones, Yousuf Karsh, H. Keyani, Suk Choo
Kim, Edward Klosterman, Jill Kohn, Stephen Kollins, Axel
Kruger, K. A. Kulczycky, Colin Lamb, James Landau,
Daniel Landiss, William Lane, Wendy Lang, Don Langson,
Claude Lanselle, Paul Lasley, James Leatherberry, Philip
Lempert, Walter Lenoir, Brenda Lewis, Russell Ley, Robert
Lipetz, Clifford Love, Robert Luce, Patrick Lyons, Wally
MacGalliard, Sandra Martin, Thomas Martinet, Harriet
Maxwell, Morton May, David McAlpin, Charles McCune,
Rosemarie McDermott, Fred McElveen, William McKit-
trick, John McQuaide, Mr. and Mrs. Robert Menschel, Otto
Meyer, Frederick Mielke Jr., Graydon Miller, Jim Miner,
Howard Minsky, Anabel Mintz, Milton Mitlas, David
Molchos, Jack Moore, James Moore, Steven Moore, James
Moorhead, Barbara & Aaron Morrison, Monte Nagler,
David Nasaw, Beatrice Nemlaha, T. T. Newbold, Scott
Nichols, Pamela Niedermayer, Jeremy Nissel, Louise
O'Connor, Thomas Parker, Kenneth Patterson, Suzanne
Paulson, Clark Perry, Tom Philbrook, Photography by
Bordeaux, Durk Piersma, Lance Prather, Marcia Reed,
Ellen Reiss, Richard Reventlow, Alfred Revzin, Alan
Richards, Gene Roberts, Ronald Rogers, Fred and Barbara
Roll, Alan Ross, Richard Ross, Ed Rountree, Mrs. George
Rowland, Noel Rubaloff, Melvine Rubin, David Ruder-
man, Bill Rusher, David Ruttenberg, Albert Santoni, Mike
Sata, John Scarlata, Tennyson Schad, John Schaefer, Fred
Scheel, Thomas Schiff, Elliott Schnackenberg, Samuel
Frank Schoninger, Jon Seidel, Eric and Jessica Shaver,
Elena Sheehan, Richard Shenk, Stephen Shepard, Martin
Shickman, David Shipman, Ralph Shishido, Rocky
Shugart, John and Ann Simpson, Mrs. Joseph Singer,
Thressa Sira, Marshall Siskin, Herb Sklar, Howard Sloane,
Joshua Smith, Frank Spadarella, Anthony Spare, Gery
Sperling, Lucia Spurgen, Peter Stamats, Alan Stamm,
George Steeves, Michael Stein, Charles Stern, Diana
Stevenson, H. N. Stevenson, Thomas Stevenson, Robert
Stiegler, William Stolze, Martin Sugg, Rodney Susholtz, W.
Douglas Swan, Barry Swift, Thomas E. Talo, Rev. and Mrs.
Jo Tartt Jr., Missy Taylor, Stephen Taylor, Margaret The,
Don Tostenrud, Jean Tucker, Dr. and Mrs. Tuerk, Robert
Tyson, Stanford Ullner, Susan Unterberg, Mrs. Thomas
Unterberg, John Upton, Grant Velie, David Vena, Joan
Vermeulen, Jack Waltman, Jonathan Wasserberger, Char-
lotte Watts, William Wenzlau, Margaret Weston, Allen
White, Randall White, Michael Wiley, Michael Wilson,
Alvin Wong, Bill Wright, David Zauel

CORPORATE MEMBERS

Calumet Photographic, Eastman Kodak, Gardner/Ful-
mer Lithograph, Victor Hasselblad, Inc., Hill Publications,
Hope Industries, Harry Lunn Gallery, Minolta Corporation, Nikon, Petersen's Photographic, Polaroid Foundation, Scheel Hardware and Sporting Goods, Schneider
Corporation of America, The Weston Gallery.

CONTRIBUTING & PATRON MEMBERS
AND SPONSORS

Joel Bernstein, Shirley Burden, Robert DeMaio, Elliot
Doft, Betty Freeman, Tina Freeman, Arnold Gartner,
Geoffrey Goldberg, Andrea Gray, Richard A. Harrison,
Marilyn Hillman, David H. McAlpin, J. Kent Minichiello,
Dr. Fred Modern, Seeley W. Mudd, II, Robert Taub, Mr. &
Mrs. Leonard Vernon, Tanya Waddell, Jane Reese
Williams, W. P. Wright, Anonymous.

TRUSTEES

Ansel Adams, Robert H. Baker, Morley Baer, Peter C.
Bunnell, Robert K. Byers, Barbara Crane, David Gardner,
Connie Glenn, Tim Hill, Jane Livingston, Harry Lunn, Otto
Meyer, Olivia Parker, Leland Rice, William H. Rusher,
John Schaefer, Fred Scheel, Julia Siebel, Paul Smart, Henry
Holmes Smith, Jerry Uelsmann, Leonard Vernon, Margaret
W. Weston, Jane Reese Williams.

ADVISORY TRUSTEES

Shirley Burden, Carl Chiarenza, James L. Enyeart, Henry
Gilpin, Andrea Gray, David McAlpin, Beaumont Newhall,
Jean Tucker, William A. Turnage, Jack Welpott.

STAFF

James Alinder, Executive Director; David Featherstone,
Executive Associate; Mary Virginia Swanson, Executive
Assistant; Peter Andersen, Production Manager; Nancy
Ponedel, Membership Secretary; Debbie Bradburn, Admin-
istrative Assistant.